This book belongs to

_____

"Charm is deceitful and beauty is vain,
but a woman who fears the Lord,
she shall be praised."

Pv. 31:30

Better Than a
New Pair of Shoes

Cristiane Cardoso

Better Than a New Pair of Shoes

C268b

Cardoso, Cristiane.
Better than a new pair of shoes
Various messages / Cristiane Cardoso. - Rio de Janeiro :
Unipro Editora, 2007.
272 p. ; 21 cm.

ISBN 978-85-7140-471-7
1. Starting From Within. 2. From Single to Married Life.
I. Title

CDD – 248.4

GENERAL COORDINATION: Sidney S. Costa
EDITORIAL COORDINATION: Renato Cardoso and Mauro Rocha
PROOFREADERS: Evelyn Higginbotham and Christoulla Boodram
COVER: Samuel Taylor
TEXT LAYOUT: Chris Buddy

1st edition
2007

Unipro

Rio de Janeiro
Estrada Adhemar Bebiano, 3.610
Inhaúma – CEP: 20766-720
Rio de Janeiro – RJ
Tel.: + 55 21 3296-9300
www.arcauniversal.com
unipro.editora@arcauniversal.com

London
FINSBURY PARK
Rainbow Theatre
232 Seven Sisters Road
Finsbury Park London N4 3NX
Tel.: + 44 (0) 20 7686 6000
Fax: + 44 (0) 20 7686 6008
www.uckg.org
info@uckg.org

Better Than a New Pair of Shoes
Code for requests: 471-7

Contents

Acknowledgements

$\mathcal{I}$ thank my Lord Jesus, who not only guided me throughout this book, but most of all, led me to experience Him in my life and meet people that I will never forget...

My loving husband, Renato, who comes up with the greatest ideas, including this book, and is always encouraging me in troubled times, always cheering me on, and adding so much more to my life (and he also removed about 80% of all exclamation marks I used when editing this book)—I love you, my other half!!! My son, Filipe, who brought me to know myself and with that, maturity and experience I could have never gained without him—my precious son, I'd go through all the hardship again to have you!

Both my parents, Edir & Ester, for believing in me, even when I had given up on myself, and for passing the faith on to me as my one and only inheritance. You've given me all I'll ever need, thank you! My sister, Viviane, who has no clue of how special she is for me, who touched me dearly through all her struggles—no one can ever take your place, my love! My dearest little brother, Moyses, whose life helped me write and understand a little more of what a teen goes through in this world. You're so talented Mo, I love you just the way you are.

Evelyn, Sandra, Chris, and Lininha, the women of faith who despite all other responsibilities, took time to work on this book simply out of love and a spirit of servitude. Mauro and Sam, who helped me keep to my deadline, thank you for so much efficiency towards this book!

And finally, all the friends I've known throughout the Work of God: you're no longer friends, but much more than that... you're part of my own family.

Introduction

I grew up keeping loads of different diaries—daily diaries and 'angst ridden' diaries. My hardships were usually best met when I put them down on paper. Through my writing, I felt closer to God and often felt better and relieved. I guess the lonely times were to my advantage, because I ended up acquiring the habit of writing the very things I could not express with my lips.

I was raised a missionary's daughter with no planned out future, no permanent home, no life-long friends, an unusual family life, which was fine for me because we were a team. My parents spent a lot of time helping us understand the kind of sacrificial life we lived. And we loved it. I didn't really have much contact with the outside world and when I got married I was still quite young, which was something my family and I had always wanted (believe it or not).

You may wonder how a daddy's girl like me could go through so much as to come to the point of writing depressing diaries, and I wondered about that too. I always thought that I went through things in my life that didn't really make sense and that perhaps I overreacted to them. But when I look back, I realise those were the times I grew out of the bubble I lived in throughout my childhood—the one that made 'naïve' my middle name. Fortunately, I realised that for someone to be greatly used by God, he or she will have to go through all sorts of hardships, so the moulding and repairing can be done.

There will be times as you read 'Better Than a New Pair of Shoes' you may feel some of the messages in it are just too much to take in. Please don't dismay. Bear with me, and bear with yourself too. It's impossible to change from night to day in one simple reading of a book. Give yourself some time, be patient as God is patient with you, just as He has been very patient with me. There's time for everything, and now it's time to bite and chew each message slowly. You may find it may not be best to read this book from cover to cover in one go, as not all articles follow a natural sequence. Feel free to read any article, in any order you like. If you're single, I'd suggest you read the articles about marriage too so you can prepare yourself. If you're married, read the articles for the youth so you can help your children.

For someone who never thought I could be or do anything meaningful in this world, God has proven me wrong. I know this book is a collection of articles I've written in the past, but some things you'll read here could very likely change the way you see life, making you a better woman all round.

That's why, I say, it will definitely do you more good than buying a new pair of shoes!

In faith,

Cristiane Cardoso
www.cristianecardoso.com

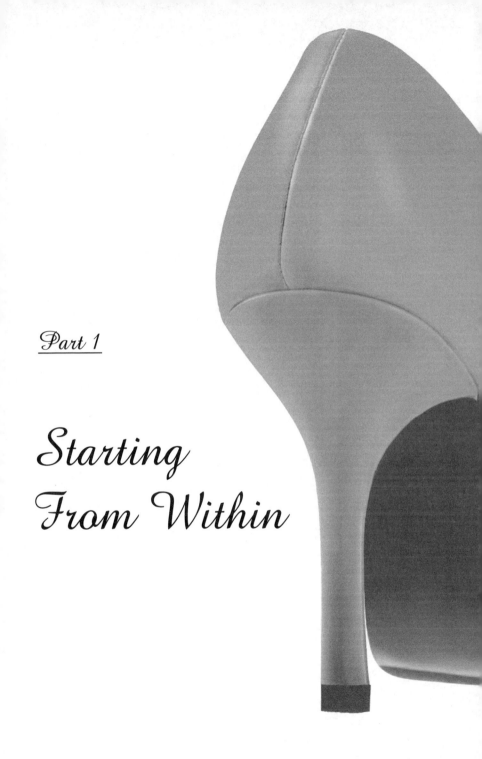

Part 1

Starting
From Within

Pretty Woman

She takes good care of herself. Her make-up is always beautifully matching her skin; her outfit is as elegant as she is; her walk is discreet and her speech genteel.

She's a pretty woman on the outside, but only God knows what goes on inside her soul. She wishes she could at least explain it to someone, but how? How can she explain her intimate sorrows? They have been with her for so long that it wouldn't even make much sense if she tried to reveal them to anyone.

It's hard to believe that a woman who apparently has it all can't be successful in the areas most needed for her to feel complete.

It's hard, but that's a reality for many pretty women nowadays. The problem is not what colour suits her best or what hairstyle is most appealing, but what to do with all that inner baggage she's carried all her life.

The baggage seems to have grown over the years. At first, it was just a word someone very close to her said one day that made her rethink how she saw herself. But as the days passed, more and more words and comments gathered together to form this baggage that she carries within. How can she break free from such an enormous load that became part of her?

First of all, not everything in that baggage is necessarily true—as a matter of fact, most likely 100% of it is a lie! Words can be spoken with a simple opening of the mouth, but they are almost never thoroughly thought through before becoming words. There are many that are spoken on the spur of the moment and these can be the most hurtful. Whatever word that has distressed you since it was spoken is not worth taking too seriously—not worth putting inside a bag and carrying it throughout your life.

Maybe what you carry within was not even caused by a word that was spoken to you. It may be just a belief you've always had—a belief that emerged from a simple idea that brought you to the wrong conclusion. Many women believe that they will never amount to anything in life. Why do they believe that? Because of the ideas they started to have about themselves very early in life. Maybe because they didn't achieve anything in school, they came to believe that they would never achieve anything. Or sometimes just because they looked in the mirror and thought they weren't as beautiful as the next girl, that idea has become a belief that they're not beautiful at all!

No matter how you have filled up your bags, when you started to fill them, or why they started getting filled, they're still bags—heavy things to be carried around. Much of what's inside them is probably unnecessary, and worst of all, you can't get very far carrying them everywhere you go! You must let go and the sooner you do, the sooner you'll become a Free Woman—the woman you were meant to be—full of potential and capable of doing extraordinary things through faith.

Life is too complicated for extra luggage! Travel light, then you can sing, "Pretty woman, walking down the street..."

Notes

_____

_____

_____

_____

_____

_____

_____

_____

A Woman's Worth

*O*nce in my life, I questioned why God had made me a woman. I thought that men were more important and that troubled me a lot. I remembered the mistakes that I often made that men almost never make. I cried to God with a bitter heart wondering about the unfairness of it all, and that was when He revealed to me my true value as a woman.

I realised that when He created Eve, He created someone special. She wasn't just one more being amongst the others He'd created, but He made woman with His own Hands, specifically to do what man could not do.

After creating man and all the animals, God still did not feel His creation was complete. It was only after He made Eve that the Lord *"looked over all He had made, and He saw that it was excellent in every way."* (Gen. 1:31) The woman completed God's creation. Her value in God's Hands was such that He gave man the commandment of leaving his own family to be united with her and to treat her as if he was taking care of his own body. Now, if women were not of much importance, why would her husband need to leave his loved ones just for her? She could have just become another member in his family with the sole purpose of taking care of him.

When the Lord Jesus came, He also gave special attention to women, at a time when women were not regarded as people of much worth. We can feel Jesus' special care when He spoke to that prostitute who had just been caught in adultery. What about His praise of that woman who washed His feet with perfume? The evidence is clear that we women have no grounds to feel unworthy or inferior to anyone. God showed this clearly through Sarah, Esther, Ruth, and many other women whom God found worthy of mention in His Word.

God made you woman, unique. Your motherly love can never be replaced. Your beauty is unique to women only. You are the light of your house and if you fall sick or travel, your home becomes dark. You can make an old flat become a "home sweet home". Your sweetness causes a flower to bloom. It's interesting to note that when a woman becomes a widow, she can live alone for the rest of her days but that is rarely the case when a man becomes a widower! A man is only complete when he has a woman of God by his side.

If you are a woman of God, know your value before Him. You were the Lord Jesus' first servant, His first witness after His resurrection, the one He wants people to remember every time His gospel is preached, and the one person He forgave, even though you had a shameful past. So look at yourself in the mirror today and see the one woman God sees from heaven—special, valued, beautiful, unique, strong, wise, hard-working, the loving wife and mother, the great homemaker, true friend and companion, faithful, honest, caring, committed, intelligent, the one whose tasks cannot be done by anyone else, they are all yours alone. Take advantage of these unique qualities and be great at them because God has chosen you and you alone!

Even if nobody shows their gratitude for the things you have done, be sure that they feel it inside more than words can express. Your husband may have left you for another woman, but only God knows how he misses your true love and care. Your children may not seem to care about your presence in the house, but in fact, you are the one person they know that has true feelings towards them. Your friends may laugh at you for being old fashioned, but boy how they wish they had your life.

I enjoyed Patrick Morley's humour in his book "What Husbands Wish Their Wives Knew About Men": "God said, 'Okay, I can see that it's not good for this man to be alone. Now how can I solve this problem? I know! I'll give Adam a pet dog and name him Rover. He will be man's best friend. No, that won't work. He needs a friend but he also needs a helper. I know what I'll do! I'll give him a workhorse. No? Maybe an ox? No, that won't work either. True, he needs a friend and a helper, but he needs someone to talk to. Hmmm... I know! I'll make another "man" and they can watch football together, talk about cars, and play golf... No, that won't work. He does need a friend and a helper and someone to talk to, but he also needs someone to help him subdue the earth... I know! I'll start a company and give him co-workers to help him care for the garden! No, no, that won't work. The garden is not the only place where the man needs help. He needs help at home, and he needs help to fill the earth with others like him. This man, look at him! He needs help everywhere! Let's see. He needs a friend so he won't be alone. He needs a helper to do his work. He needs a companion to talk to. He needs help at work and at home. And he needs a helper to make little men. Hmmm... I know! I've got it! I'll make a woman!"

We should recognise our true value, which is *"worth more than precious rubies."* (Pv. 31:10)

Notes

_____

_____

_____

_____

_____

_____

_____

_____

_____

_____

_____

_____

_____

The Woman Within

$\mathcal{T}$he greatest struggle of a woman is within her. The minute she sets out to do something major in her life, a voice deep within is heard and will continue to be heard until she finally ignores it and goes ahead with her task. Voices that say she does not deserve to be happy. Voices that say she can never be the woman she wants to be. Voices that say she will never be good enough.

If we could name these voices, we could perhaps call them inner abusive voices. If it wasn't for this daily struggle we have to go through, everything would be so much easier, much less complex, and far better. Unfortunately, they are here to stay. You and I go through this struggle everyday, all the time. Be it at home, or at work, at night, or during the day, the fight goes on for all of us.

However, in this daily battle lies the key to both success and failure of every human being. Just like in all battles, someone has to be the winner. Sometimes it's not necessarily the stronger, but the one that lasts the longest. If you think about it, the key to your success is within you. If you overcome your daily battle, you succeed in life. If you fail in your daily battle, you fail in life.

Some people think that their success depends on God alone, but wouldn't you think that if it were entirely up to Him, we would all be successful in life since He is True Love? Could a Father enjoy seeing His children suffering, depressed, losing hope in life, and miserable?

Some things in life can only be done by us, not even God can interfere. And one of these things is to fight our inner self that keeps on pulling us down, making us feel unworthy, and giving us ideas of giving up. It's a huge fight that no one ever sees. It goes on in the dark, in the deepest place of our being, and it is between YOU and the INNER YOU.

Have you ever not done something out of fear and later regretted it for many days afterwards? Have you ever given up on an idea because you thought you could never get it done yourself? Have you ever looked in the mirror and thought to yourself, "I'll never be anyone?" If so, bingo! Those were inner battles that you lost.

It doesn't only happen to some people—it happens to everybody. Born of God, filled with the Holy Spirit Christians go through this everyday and because of some failed battles, they can never truly testify to God's power in their lives. They blame the church, the pastor, the people, the government and even God—but they fail to see that the real blame is on them for not overcoming their own inner battles.

Remember Queen Esther? She must have gone through all kinds of battles within herself before going to speak to her husband the King, whose reputation was that of a furious king who didn't spare even his own ex-wife. We don't read about the thoughts that came into her head through those three days of prayer and fasting. It must have been the longest three days of her life, but she overcame herself and consequently became the heroine of Israel at the time, plus an example to all of us today. Read the book of Esther.

The battle goes on and only the strong and persistent will make it.

Notes

_____

_____

_____

_____

_____

_____

_____

_____

Best Choice

$\mathscr{A}$ll of a sudden you find yourself surrounded on all sides and there's nowhere and no one to turn to. You pray but your prayers only come out in tears and you wonder if God heard that at all. You ask for advice but no one seems to understand what you're going through. You're in a black tunnel and that light that's supposed to be at the end isn't there. Why? What have I done to deserve this? How can I go on?

Trust in God.

Isn't that one of the hardest things to do when everything is tumbling down around us? So easily taught and so hard to live, it's the only real option when dark, cloudy days, months, and years just never seem to end, when problems seem to have conspired to go on a coordinated assault against us and rise up everywhere! Gradually, we become more and more vulnerable.

Yet we still think there's something we can do or fix. It's as if we never learn our lesson. How many times have we tried to fix problems with our own hands? How many times did we succeed? Yes, go ahead, try answering that. As much as we hate to admit it, we do not have all the answers and we do need help from above. Your pastor or your best friend cannot help you—understand this. Your help can only come from above.

That's what Hannah realised after so many years of pitying herself for not having any children. She had the love of her husband, but still lived in shame. She couldn't even eat anymore. The more time passed, the more shame seemed to drown her, until the day she decided to go to God directly. Yearly, she would offer the double portion her husband would give her to sacrifice to God, but this time she offered something of herself—something that belonged to her.

She broke down in tears and words only came out in groans of pain, but she still made the vow that changed her life: *"O LORD of hosts, if You will indeed look on the affliction of Your maidservant and remember me, and not forget Your maidservant, but will give Your maidservant a male child, then I will give him to the LORD all the days of his life..."* (1 Sa. 1:11) Hannah sacrificed the one thing she wanted most in her life—the right to be a mother.

Hannah finally trusted in God enough to pray and leave her burdens in His Hands and more—she sacrificed her dream! She truly trusted in Him this time, for even if He gave her what she wanted the most in her life, she'd give it back to Him. The Bible relates that, "the woman went her way and ate, and her face was no longer sad." (1 Sa. 1:18) She trusted in God.

God answered Hannah by giving her a son that truly honoured Him, a great man of God called Samuel, for He saw her trust and willingness to let go of one of the most precious things in her life, just so she could honour Him.

Hannah's trust is what we need to feed into our heart, be it in our love life, family, or health. It is of no use to have so much faith and lack the one thing that holds it up—trust. Trust God with your problems and don't let them get the best of you. Eat and let your face no longer be sad.

Notes

The Bridge

There is a cry deep within every woman—a sad story to tell, a disappointing experience to vent, and a past we wish would disappear. We all have a story that took time to complete and if we wrote about it, it would be a bestseller.

There are marks everywhere in our hearts. Marks that became scars with time. Nobody understands, and how can they? These marks were personal and deep. People can never understand what goes on inside other people's hearts. It is an unknown place, and the scars can't help but make it seem even scary.

Whenever a sad song or a specific comment is heard, it's hard to contain the tears that come all the way from the dark corners of our hearts. Some women try to cope with these sad memories by trying to forget about them, although, they themselves know that such a big scar that practically deformed them can't be ignored. Some other women live in a constantly depressed state, as if life was a burden to wake up to everyday.

As much as we don't like to admit it, every real woman of God goes through hardships in her life. Disappointments, hurts, ungratefulness, humiliation, rejection, scorn, and loneliness are just a few of the paths we travel on throughout our lives in order to become stronger and more mature. It's like a long, wobbly bridge that we have to cross to get to a better state of mind. And throughout this journey over the bridge, we are scratched, we are bruised, and sometimes, we can even break a leg.

By the time we get to the other side of this enormous old bridge, we have become completely different women. We have scars all over us and yet we have a sense of strength within. Strength that we did not acquire from books or articles for women, but solely through our own experiences.

Yet, not all of us get to the other side of this bridge at the same time. Some get there faster than others because each time they fall or get hurt throughout their journey, they learn to do it better next time and are more cautious. Others though, keep on falling and hurting themselves and still don't learn from their mistakes. So they keep on getting hurt, and keep lagging behind.

The stronger a woman is, the farther she'll get on this bridge. She falls like everyone else, but she quickly recovers and continues her journey. The wiser a woman is, the faster she'll reach at the end of this bridge because she doesn't waste time looking at how others are crossing their own bridges.

And when we finally cross this bridge, there's another one a mile down the road, in worse shape and harder than the last. That's how life is, either we're overcomers or we're losers. Some people like to stay in between bridges so they won't be hurt again, but that only means they won't go very far in life.

The more scars we have, the stronger and more successful we are. Women who avoid scars will never be the women they want to be in life because every good thing comes at a price. The better it is, the more expensive the price we have to pay.

Notes

_____

_____

_____

_____

_____

_____

_____

Dealing With Problems

Sometimes life is like a nightmare. Everything that happens also ceases to happen after some time. Just when you think your hardships are over, another kind of hardship comes along. The fact is that everything passes, good and bad. The only thing that really stays is the person herself—her character, reputation, and strength.

It's all but a theory when the actual problem is at hand. It just doesn't seem to ever go away, but you and I know that eventually it will. The real problem is how we handle the problem. Many are those that let the problem take over their lives, leading them straight to anti-depressants. Others let the problem lead them into making more problems for themselves.

I remember a young lady who was very anti-men. She was not a lesbian, but she was determined to live without fulfilment in her love life. When asked why she had developed such hatred for men, she gave the perfect excuse: men had abused her in the past and so she could not trust another one ever again. The sad reality about this young lady is that because of a bad experience in her past, she decided to destroy her future as well. In other words, the problem led her into making more problems for herself.

Many people don't have a clue how to deal with their problems. They choose the hardest paths to handle them and few truly take advantage of their problems. You see, problems can also be blessings in disguise. Of course, they will often make us cry or be very upset, and can even lead us to humiliation and stress. Nevertheless, those who know how to react positively to their problems can actually turn them into blessings!

Instead of reacting negatively to the problem, try to understand the problem. Instead of crying about it, do some thinking about it.

There's always something there you missed that could very much be the key to never going through the same problem again in your life—for instance, a bad marriage. Some women get themselves into a bad marriage, but if they really think about it, they'll realise that before marrying the wrong husband, there were signs showing that he was the wrong choice.

It was his sudden shifts of temper, or his constant disagreeing, or his closeness to single women, or his too close relationship with his relatives, or his inability to finish whatever he started, or his difficulty to find a permanent job, and so on. Women tend to think that these things will change after marriage, when in fact, they often get worse!

If you want to know if your marriage will run smoothly, see how your period of courtship has been. Has it been rocky? Then your marriage will be earthquakey. Was it smooth and a bed of roses? Then your marriage will most probably work!

Take advantage of your problems—see what they really mean, read between the lines, and make sure you learn the lesson. This is what problems are all about. They're there for us to learn from and do better next time—that's all. Don't give your problem so much power by sinking into depression or destroying a whole future ahead of you because of what happened. Otherwise, it will keep on happening until you learn your lesson.

Notes

_____

_____

_____

_____

_____

_____

_____

_____

The Shunammite Dream

There was a Shunammite woman who lived in the time of the prophet Elisha. She was married to a rich man who feared God and they both served Him with their lives and offerings. But there was something special about this woman that differentiated her from all the other Shunammite women in her time—she was gracious. This woman of grace wasn't only gracious to those she loved, and that was what caught the attention of God.

The prophet Elisha, the man of God, always passed through her town, and this woman always offered him food every time he came through. One day she realised that she could do something more. She agreed with her husband to build him a room so that he could rest whenever he passed by her town.

The prophet was surprised at her gracious attitude, seeing that she wasn't gaining anything by it, and he felt obliged to bless her some-how. He then asked her what she would like to receive from God. However, the Shunammite woman wasn't doing this for blessings or to receive anything in return. This attitude had come from an honest desire to be gracious. She knew that whatever she did for the man of God, she was actually doing for God, and so she didn't hesitate to spend some of her money, time, and work in order to do this.

The man of God wasn't satisfied with that answer and so he asked around and found out that this gracious woman did not have any children. It must have been this woman's dream to have children of her own but because her husband was advanced in age, she had already lost all hope. Elisha didn't think twice in blessing her with the one thing she had never had and yet dreamed of all her life—a child. Read about this in 2 Kings 4:8-17.

Here we see the example of a woman who received a big blessing without asking for it just because of her different kind of spirit. This woman stood out from all other women in her time, so much so that the Bible makes sure her story is mentioned. We women have opportunities everyday to stand out and make a difference and yet, why is it that so few of us can actually do it?

Opportunities come every time an idea comes into mind. The problem is what we do with these ideas. Sometimes they're taken lightly, other times, they're forgotten and thought of as foolish. If only we took each of them one at a time and considered them as opportunities to stand out and be gracious! The man of God was always passing by the Shunammite woman's town and so she decided to take it as an opportunity of a lifetime (even though she didn't even realise it at that moment).

One of the most beautiful characteristics of a woman is her ability to be graceful. Every woman is born with this ability. Unfortunately, not all go to the extent of actually using it for the benefit of others. Many think that if they're indifferent to people's needs, they'll avoid bringing problems to themselves. Others are too worried of what people will think and others simply don't take the time to look around because they're so focused on their own lives.

No wonder only the *"...gracious woman retains honour."* (Pr. 11:16)

Notes

_____

_____

_____

_____

_____

_____

_____

_____

A True Friend

A true friend is like a jewel. You keep it safe and you'll always have it. You don't get tired of it or feel like giving it away. It had a cost, a very high one, and it's exclusively for you. It probably reminds you of some good occasion or someone special in your life.

So is a true friend. People who live their lives thinking that friends aren't that important are people who never had one. They may have so-called "friends", but not a true friend.

A true friend is always there for you, even when you're mad or angry. She admires you and therefore makes you feel good about yourself. One of her best moments is when you're the star. And when you're not in the mood, she still understands.

It may sound too good to be true, but it's true when you have a true friend. Few people have true friends because they're hard to find. Not everyone is willing to see you happier than they. In fact, few people enjoy seeing other people's happiness.

The Lord Jesus was and is a True Friend. He volunteered Himself before God to leave His heavenly post and come down and become nothing so that we could become something. Then He lived day and night evangelising and preaching the good news to people everywhere, so much so that sometimes He didn't have time to eat. And what did He often get in return? Misunderstanding, judgement, criticism, and disdain.

Still He didn't stop giving. He went on giving more and more of Himself until the day He had to give His own life. And to think that still today there are those who have a low opinion of the Lord Jesus and say He was just a prophet or a wise man. It's just unbelievable!

His giving didn't stop there either. He died and resurrected and with all the glory and honour of being a true HERO (that's what I call a HERO!), He continues giving to those who call upon Him. People who did all sorts of wrong, prostitutes, adulterers, thieves, murderers, and even terrorists. Anyone who calls upon His Name and by faith gives his life to Him, receives a chance to start it all over again and live life to the fullest.

The bigger the sinner, the greater His pleasure to restore him/her to a new life. Now, where can you find

a better Friend? Why go on living in loneliness when you could have a True Friend by your side at all times—one who's a true HERO! Who's worthy of all the awards and more? One who loves you for who you are and will never leave you or forsake you!

Why think that He has forsaken you whilst He's the only One who hasn't? Why think that He's not there when He's actually the only One around?

Notes

_____

_____

_____

_____

_____

_____

_____

_____

_____

_____

_____

_____

_____

No. 1 Quality

The Lord Jesus gave. He didn't just give us words and bless-ings—He gave us His life. Now for some people, this is an overused expression just like, "Oh My God". They hear it so many times that it just doesn't really affect them anymore.

When I think of the word "give", I can relate to some good and bad experiences in my life. People give you a smile or a head to toe look, a compliment or a stab in the back, a thank you or a silent rejection, time of day or a simple "not now". We're always either giving or receiving and in doing so, we're always either making someone happy or unhappy.

Our human nature is that of using people, getting the best out of them, and living our selfish lives for ourselves. Fortunately, God has given us a way to have His own nature. A holy nature that gives, no matter what.

One of the greatest qualities in a woman of God is her pleasure in giving her best without receiving anything in return. Not that other women won't give, but there's a big difference between her and the other women who don't have God's nature in them.

The woman of God will give you her time for free whilst the oth-ers will charge you for it. She will give you a compliment whilst the others will roll their eyes soon after giving one. She will give you a gift whilst the others will surely give you a gift, but only if they're getting something in return. She will give even when she cannot, whilst the others will simply not go that extra mile—even when they can.

She will sometimes lack so you can have—and lose so you can gain. But isn't that what our Lord did for us? Think of everything He's gone through so that we would be here today. Many people haven't recognised His existence in their lives and they just go after His blessings, but still, He will give them what they want, even knowing that they're just using Him.

Give and you shall receive—but not just a blessing here and there. You'll receive more than you have ever asked for; you'll receive Him for all your life. No more loneliness. Though everyone may leave you, you'll still have Him. He'll be your Husband when one is not there for you. He'll be your Friend even when all your friends misunderstand you. He'll be your Guide when you are confused; He'll be Everything you've always wanted in life.

Give Him your life—what you think, what you want, and what you feel. From the moment you do this, you'll have His nature in you.

No need to study or take a course to do that. Just give and you'll RECEIVE! When His nature is in you, you'll give to others and you'll truly feel blessed—and you'll understand why it's better to give than to receive.

Notes

_____

_____

_____

_____

_____

_____

_____

_____

_____

_____

_____

_____

_____

Dear Woman of God

There is something that you might be missing out on in your journey to a fulfilled life which is extremely important for you to succeed. Life is not as complicated as we think. There's always a choice to be made and depending on which one we choose, life won't need to be so hard.

You might be thinking that it's easy for me to say this as I am not in your shoes, and I completely understand your point, but think with me—what choices did you make in order to be where you are today? What if you had made another choice, do you think things would still have turned out this way for you?

Everything in life depends on a simple choice. Even the little things, the every day things, the things that we can't possibly imagine are going to change your whole life. For instance, you have a choice of either getting angry or not, answering back or not, turning away or not, accepting life as it comes at you or not, changing or not, committing or not, being responsible or not, and so on. Life is about choices—if we make the right ones, we'll end up where we want. That's how simple it is.

Now you may wonder how on earth would you know which choice to make at the time when things seem to be so blurry and dark? And that's where faith comes in. When we use faith instead of emotions, we can see things that are not yet apparent to the human eye. Emotions, on the other hand, make us see things as they seem, not as they are, and that's when we end up making the wrong choice.

If you could only look ahead in time, would you have made the same choices? Faith looks ahead. Faith is "to believe in something you cannot see or touch", in the uncertain future, in the impossible, physically speaking.

Not all women of God walk by faith. Many started walking by faith but are now walking by what they see, touch, and feel. They live in a weak state of mind, full of doubts and insecurities. They are always in need of someone to push them forward, to boost their self-confidence, and to motivate them to continue fighting. It's not a matter of how you were brought up or what you've been through, it's a matter of faith. Either you live by it or you don't.

Of all the advice I got in my life, the strongest and most effective one up to this date was the one my father gave me on how to live by faith. Throughout my life, besides all the good things that God has given me,

I have often been disappointed, rebuked, humiliated, taken for granted, used, and harshly criticised and yet, I have nothing that holds me back. No grudge or any kind of extra luggage, just because I chose not to carry them and simply live by faith.

There will always be setbacks, but we can either use them to boost our faith and do better next time, or just let them take us down for good. It's the exceptional choice and you can still make it despite what you've been through. There's always another chance to start again. God gives us this opportunity every day we wake up as the sun rises (here in London, above the clouds...). That may well be the reason why we have day and night—so there will always be another day to start again!

Notes

_____

_____

_____

_____

_____

_____

_____

Blah, Blah, Blah

So there she was, fed up and quite depressed, too. The situation at home was getting out of hand and her patience had its limits. She knew that it wasn't because of the lack of prayers and vows made before God, because she had been doing this for years now. Things didn't seem to be getting anywhere. Her husband was still unemployed, her son on drugs, and her daughter going out with the wrong crowd.

All her friends and relatives already knew about it because this woman just felt it was too hard to hold it all inside whenever anyone, and I mean, ANYONE, asked her how things were. It was as if her limits had already been exceeded! "When will I ever get a break?" She'd sob over and over again, in the shower, on the bus, and anywhere, every time she remembered her family.

Isn't that the way many of us react to persistent problems? When we don't see any change after doing so much, we feel frustrated with time, and how hard it seems to see even a small change.

Faith doesn't work within a time limit. Faith is a belief, and if you can hold on to it when everything around you is contrary to your belief, you're using your faith. It's a matter of trust. That is what many people find difficult to understand about faith. It can't be understood. It's faith!

They receive a strong prayer now and as they go back to their seat or home, they're looking for proof of that prayer. When none can be "felt" or "touched", they quickly disregard that strong prayer as just one more that didn't work. Little do they know that they're losing their blessing right then and there, when they allow circumstances around to "prove" their faith wrong.

The person immediately gets into a state of complaining. "Nothing ever happens to me", "There must be something wrong with me or this church", "Why doesn't God answer my prayers?" and the spiritual nagging goes on and on. It first starts in the mind, the thoughts that come from everywhere and everyone but God. Then the chaos in the mind gets so out of hand that the person can hardly hold it all, and then all that pressure is vented on everyone around.

The complaining and nagging about the delay of our blessings are actually ways to hold back the blessings from coming altogether. Every time we complain about something with anyone else besides God, we actually doubt that He's in control of our lives. If we believe, it doesn't matter how long it's taking or how things seem to be going, we will continue trusting that our Lord is in control.

But you may say, "Sometimes, it's just too hard! I have to vent it somehow!" which is fair, but why express it to people who can do nothing about it? If you have to express it, then tell it to God—complain to Him, tell Him and only Him your frustrations, because after all, isn't He the One you're depending on?

Moses had always complained to God concerning his problems, and God delighted in his dependence on Him. But one day, he complained to the people (read Numbers 20.10) about the miracle that God was about to perform and that was it for him—he lost his right to enter the Promised Land. A simple nagging, a great loss!

Notes

_____

_____

_____

_____

_____

_____

_____

_____

Cindy's Faith

Today, Cindy used her faith. After a troubled day yesterday, she went to sleep feeling like the worst person in the world. She simply wanted to die and contemplated how things would be if she had simply disappeared from the face of the earth. That was the longest night of her life and for a moment, she was even feverish. Nevertheless, Cindy woke up with a determination in her heart that she was going to change and not only that, she was going to fix all the damage she caused to the relationships she most valued in her life.

The first thing she did was to recognise her problem. All problems she had recently with people around her had in some way or the other been her fault. She felt as if she was standing in front of a number of people saying, "My name is Cindy and I have a bad temper." She knew that she couldn't skip this first step, after all, if things were going to change, she would have to deal with the root of the problem.

She then took another step towards change. She apologised to the one she hurt the most. That must have been one of the hardest actions to take. She could hardly look straight into her brother's eyes, because it was too humiliating for any eye contact. However, the feeling she had after taking that step, although extremely difficult, was one of the most pleasant ones she had ever had. She was actually proud of herself!

Truly she knew that if change was going to come, she would have to take the next big step, which was actually changing her attitude. All those thoughts that she kept pondering the night before now seemed to be fake; she concluded then that her inability to change was also untrue and that she was going to make it happen one day at a time. So she changed. It was as simple as that! We conclude that if one wants to change, all one's got to do is actually CHANGE!

It is inevitable that in the beginning, she would still fail here and there, but if she took that as proof that change was impossible, then she would be lost. So, Cindy gave herself another chance, but this time a realistic one. She knew that she would have to take one day at a time. Failing again does not prove that change is impossible. The only time that change is impossible is when we decide it is!

Cindy was determined and because of that, everything started to turn upside down. It's funny how certain problems come the minute one decides to change. Criticism and misunderstanding were just a few of the problems standing in the queue for her to deal with. Nevertheless, she used her faith not to let all those hardships take her down. It wasn't easy and tears were rolling everywhere. There was a time she even asked herself, "Why is all this happening to me?"

Cindy used her faith and therefore is still standing, looking forward to another day of doing and practising what she believes in. And what's great about it is that Cindy is not in the Bible or in a book somewhere but living today as you read her story.

Notes

The Vicious Cycle

How on earth would anyone take over a school and terrorise children in the name of justice? Or how can a beautiful girl grow up to become a prostitute and serial killer? Or how can two young teenagers full of potential commit suicide together?

Nothing can justify the terrible things some people do, but it is also fair to say that nothing can justify what they have been through either. The whole world is appalled by what those "black widows" have done. Moviemakers named this young prostitute killer "Monster." And then there are the deaths of the two English girls that made news in the UK. All their wrongdoings were merely reactions to their own personal injustices, and it's all part of a cycle.

They go through injustice early in life, then they cause injustice to others, then others go through injustice early in life, then they cause injustice to others, and the cycle repeats itself again and again, through every generation, century after century.

The more we try to live life as we think is best, as we think will make a difference, and as we think is just and right, the farther away we drift from God. Not because He doesn't want us to have our own opinions and views, but because He knows better. After all, how old are we? Could we ever imagine comparing ourselves to Someone who's been there forever?

When we read about these women, we tend to judge them, but the reality is that these women lived with injustice all their lives. God was there with them at all times but He wasn't called upon—they didn't believe that He could change their situation, but instead they blamed Him and thought they had been born to suffer.

God is a Just God. His will is for your own good. Do you believe that? If you say you do but often feel angry at Him, and the thought of giving up is constantly tempting you, then the answer is no—you don't believe He's there for you and you don't believe He wants the best for you.

Remember when you were young and you periodically hated a decision your parents made for you? If you're a grown-up today, you probably thank God about that decision, after all, at the time it didn't seem right, but now you realise you were so immature then.

Now multiply that experience by 100 and it might be close to what you go through with God. He knows what's best for you. It's no use giving up or living in anger daily, making other peoples' lives miserable by your attitudes or revenge tactics. It's not your child's fault that your husband is not around. It's not your parent's fault that you didn't succeed in life. And above all, it's not God's fault!

So come to God and let Him help you. He'll avenge your cause. He'll do justice in your life. He'll show you why you were carefully chosen whilst still in your mother's womb.

Notes

_____

_____

_____

_____

_____

_____

_____

_____

_____

_____

_____

_____

Forsaken Women

*B*eautiful and full of life, these women live past their struggles and hardships, so that the name of the Lord Jesus may be glorified. They go from desperation to shame and humiliation and loneliness, but they keep their faith, with a strong determination inside their soul that nothing and no one will ever remove them from the presence of their Maker.

God has become their husband. The One who remained, the One who cared enough, the One who understood, the One who did not change, the One who will always be there no matter how old or how out of shape they become, He is the One Person they know will stick with them until the day they die.

These women are the ones closest to God for He is the only One they have, and because of that they become strong pillars in the Church of the Lord Jesus Christ. Their strength exceeds everyone's expectations, despite everything that has happened to them, and so they show a life that is not moved by emotions but by faith revealing their righteousness before God, *"...The just shall live by his faith."* (Hab. 2:4)

They are not looking for pity or comfort from anyone. They're looking for ways to serve God even in the midst of turbulence, desperation, and abandonment. They have one goal in life and that is to serve the Lord who also went through much turbulence, desperation, and abandonment on their behalf.

Forsaken by their very husbands, they are now women who are true examples of faith in the Lord Jesus Christ showing Him and everybody else that their faith does not depend on any "terms of agreement", but is alive no matter what happens.

"'For your Maker is your husband, the Lord of hosts is His name; and your Redeemer is the Holy One of Israel; He is called the God of the whole earth. For the Lord has called you like a woman forsaken and grieved in spirit, like a youthful wife when you were refused, says your God. For a mere moment I have forsaken you, but with great mercies I will gather you. With a little wrath I hid My face from you for a moment; But with everlasting kindness I will have mercy on you,' says the Lord, your Redeemer... 'So have I sworn that I would not be angry with you, nor rebuke you. For the mountains shall depart and the hills be removed, but My kindness shall not depart from you, nor shall My covenant of peace be removed' says the Lord, who has mercy on you. 'O you afflicted one, tossed with tempest, and not comforted, behold I will lay your stones with colourful gems, and lay your foundations with sapphires. I will make your pinnacles of rubies, your gates of crystal, and all your walls of precious stones. All your children shall be taught by the Lord, and great shall be the peace of your children. In righteousness you shall be established; you shall be far from oppression, for you shall not fear; and from terror, for it shall not come near you. Indeed, they shall surely assemble, but not because of Me. Whoever assembles against you shall fall for your sake... No weapon formed against you shall prosper, and every tongue which rises against you in judgement you shall condemn. This is the heritage of the servants of the Lord, and their righteousness is from Me' says the Lord." (Isa. 54:5-17)

Notes

_____

_____

_____

_____

_____

_____

_____

Are You a Tired Christian?

Rainy days come and go, and sometimes we can even get used to them, but not when the rain is pouring down and everything around seems grey and sad. You want to go to sleep and only wake up next month to give plenty of time for it all to disappear. Every now and again, this feeling comes to mind, especially at a certain time of the month—when 75% of our being is pure emotions!

But as soon as the grey skies are gone, we wonder why we made such a big deal out of it in the first place. What were we thinking when the idea of disappearing from the face of the earth was so constant in our minds? Why do we make such a big deal out of small things we find here and there?

Our Lord knew this when He once said, *"Take My yoke upon you and learn from Me, for I am gentle and lowly in heart, and you will find rest for your souls. For My yoke is easy and My burden is light."* (Mt. 11:29 - 30) He knew how dramatic we can be sometimes, especially when things just seem to be going against us, and yet His amazing patience in taking our burdens in His Hands whenever we come to Him can be so rewarding.

You'd think that being a Christian would be another unnecessary yoke upon you—as if we'd have to be this perfect holy person separate from everybody else in the world. But here in this verse, our Lord says, *"My yoke is easy and My burden is light"*! Why do Christians feel so overburdened then? So much pressure from this religion or that church—what's wrong then?

Our Lord is gentle and lowly in heart. He said we can find rest for our soul and that His yoke is easy. If you ever feel pressured or burdened because of anything going on in your life, all you need to do is leave it all in His Hands. He will not demand anything that you cannot do. He's patient and if you don't have the strength to change everything about yourself at once, He'll give you that strength and little by little, when you're ready to take another step towards Him, His open arms will welcome you.

This is the Christian life I know. Everything else that is said about Christianity, that imposes and demands things of people in such a way that it seems as if we were prisoners, are unnecessary burdens that can sometimes drive people away from God. God wants to help, not drive you away. He wants to add and not take away the partial peace you hold onto so tight. His burden is light so that whenever you're too weak to use your faith, He won't judge you, but instead, will guide you through the paths you need to get rid of this situation.

Think of Him as a Loving Father. Someone that is there for you no matter what. You've done something terrible? He's still taking your side, though He might not agree with what you've done, He'll help you get out of the rut you may have fallen into. Stop placing such a burden and yoke upon yourself—His yoke is easy and His burden is light. Doesn't that say it all?

Notes

_____

_____

_____

_____

_____

_____

_____

_____

_____

_____

_____

_____

A New Day Has Come

Do you know that tight feeling inside your heart that hurts and is too heavy to let you get anything done that day? You know, the thought that it's too late to change now and the horrible assurance that you probably will never change is knocking at the door? Your own voice turns against you, saying, "Now you've done it, it's over!" and all you want to do is do nothing all day long. Going to work is too hard, smiling at someone is just impossible, and getting up from your bed is just out of the question. If you could only undo that or just delete it altogether, but now it's in the past and will stay there forever and you feel like you'll never be the same ever again.

Constantly trying and failing again and again, spoils your will to face any future trials and so this negative response to life is very common: you think it's all useless and that you'll never change. But the truth is that you never really started again. The simple fact of saying you'll start again and that things will be different next time around is not enough. Something is missing. Determination is also not enough—you may be determined for a period, but there will certainly be another phase when you won't be. A whole new beginning needs to happen—something that will make you change dramatically, something that makes everything that has passed be just part of the past, and not part of who you are.

When God created everything, He was very specific about day and night. He could have left it always as day, couldn't He? The day is much better for everyone; it's much safer to live in the day-light, but still He chose to make day and night separate from each other. There can be many reasons for this, but one of the strongest ones for you and me is the fact that everyday can be a new beginning. There's always going to be a day after a whole night. And God's mercy renews itself every day. Now, can you imagine that? Can you fully understand the newness of life you can have with God?

While people don't give you a second chance, God gives you a third chance! That's right, it doesn't matter what you have done, what you have been, and what you have said. He's not like people that keep on reminding you of what you've done wrong—but instead, He understands why you did that, why you were that way, and even why you said all that—and all He wants from you is to leave your past behind you and start a new life with Him. It is not that hard, think about it. It's like deleting a whole chapter of your book and writing a new one from scratch.

You have tried to start again, to change, and do things differently before, but they have never succeeded because you were doing it by yourself—and even with all the determination you have inside you, it's almost impossible to forgive yourself. But God forgives you. He doesn't want to hear about it anymore. He just wants to plan new things ahead with you. Now all you have to do is to want it and give Him the go ahead.

Notes

A Broken Friendship

Friendship is one of life's necessities for every man and woman. It starts right when you're born, when you first feel the warmth of your sweet mother holding you so tight that you don't want her to let go. It goes on as you grow a little older and you first learn how to make your father laugh. Then as you are old enough to go to school, you meet this other girl your age who seems to be everything you've always wanted to be. And as you become an adult, you marry the man of your dreams who becomes your best friend. Unfortunately, this scenario is from an ideal world as this is not how it turns out for everyone.

Friends come and go, friendships start and finish, and best friends can sometimes let distance get between them. Most of the time, we are the ones allowing this break-up to happen. Some gossip you listened to, a misunderstanding, an attitude without thinking, and an expectation higher than anyone could possibly achieve. We know how friendship is important to us but when little things such as these come between us and a friend, we quickly forget their importance in our lives and quickly make the usual choice: distance.

Have you ever heard of distance healing a wound? The wound in the heart cannot be healed with distance or time because it's something from within, and memories just don't disappear like that. "Time heals all wounds" but do you know what that truly means? It doesn't mean that if you distance yourself from the person who hurt you, your wounds will be healed, because if it did, where do grudges come from?

It means that when time passes, and one finally concludes how foolish it is to hold onto bad memories about someone, she is finally healed. Grudges don't harm anyone but you. When you hold something bad inside, it goes with you everywhere you go like an unnecessary burden hanging around your neck. If you think about it, why carry it with you if you could just put it down and move on?

I had two very close friends once who distanced themselves because of circumstances all around, and at the time, I felt really hurt. Every time I heard their names, I'd remember how disappointed they made me feel and I would often not be interested in what people had to say about one or the other. I had already forgiven them in my heart, but I decided never to let myself be hurt that way again, and so I distanced myself as well.

It was only then God spoke to me that it is useless to treat them the way they were treating me, because that way, I'd be in the wrong just as they were. Why would I allow others to influence me to do things I don't normally do just so I'd protect myself? How often in order to protect ourselves, do we end up doing the same wrong thing as the other person did by distancing ourselves, changing towards them, and even looking at them in a different way?

In my heart, I had always tried to be such a good friend, why would I now do otherwise? This is why broken friendships happen: we let them break. If we remain a good friend, the friendship will not be broken and we will end up being the one teaching the lesson.

Notes

_____

_____

_____

_____

_____

_____

_____

_____

_____

Killing Softly With Words

Words are here to stay. The minute you say them out loud, you're actually writing them down on someone's heart, and sometimes, a person will live her whole life upon those words.

What have you said to your loved one today? With what kind of words have you marked his heart and mind up to this day? I know that sometimes it's hard to control ourselves, especially in those moments of pure anger. But is it worth destroying someone's self-esteem over something so small that they've done?

God tolerates our stubborn hearts day after day and still He won't destroy us with words. On the contrary, He's always saying something good to us—how we can always start again (Isaiah 43:18,19), that He'll never forget us (Isaiah 49:15), He'll always be there for us (Matthew 28:20), that His love is unconditional (Romans 8:35), that we're the apple of His Eyes (Zechariah 2:8), that our names are written on the palm of His Hands (Isaiah 43:16).

Besides having to deal with our own problems and doubts from the devil disturbing our minds, we still have to tolerate more words, more doubts, more misunderstanding that are just slowly killing us. Many have given up on life because they couldn't take it anymore—husbands have left, wives have gone back to their parents' home, children have gone into drugs and alcohol, all in the name of words that shouldn't have been said.

These words that keep on issuing from the mouth can be worse than murder. When you die there's no aftermath or trauma to carry, but with words, you die within and struggle to live on the outside. You have to cope to live your whole life with all those words in the back of your mind; it's a burden no one should have to carry. Words can be like bullets to the soul. I have lost count of the times

I've spoken to women who have all it takes to succeed, but don't because of what someone said or labelled them with. They can be the most beautiful women and yet all they can see is ugliness staring at them in the mirror.

One of the best ways to avoid putting this burden on others is to never speak when you're angry or full of emotions because it's almost impossible to filter your words in these circumstances. Let things calm down, perhaps you will want to speak the next day or later in the week—and if you still feel that you're not quite ready to speak, don't.

Dealing with your children, for example, can be tough sometimes as you have the responsibility to teach and correct them. But remember, your words are stronger than anyone else's for them. They can tolerate bullies, but they can't tolerate their own mother's destructive words!

Let's listen more and speak less! *"He who guards his mouth preserves his life, but he who opens wide his lips shall have destruction."* (Pv. 13:3)

Notes

_____

_____

_____

_____

_____

_____

_____

_____

_____

_____

_____

Knowing Your Place

It's frustrating to hear about the constant acts of terrorism between Arab countries and Israel, and it's even more frustrating to realise that their enmity began back in the days of Abraham.

Sarah didn't really want to wait for God's provision of a son of her own, so she, like most of us, thought of a plan on how to get what she wanted in a quicker and easier way. So she agreed with her servant girl, Hagar, to get pregnant by Abraham on her behalf and later on, to adopt her child as her own. Hagar agreed and so did Abraham.

Nevertheless, as soon as Hagar found herself pregnant with her master's child, she thought of the great advantages she now had, after all, her master's child was hers too. She then started to look down on Sarah, despising the fact that it was because of Sarah that she was now pregnant with Abraham's child.

It's like that proverb in the Bible: *"For three things the earth is perturbed, yes, for four it cannot bear up: for a servant when he reigns, a fool when he is filled with food, a hateful woman when she is married, and a maidservant who succeeds her mistress."* (Pv. 30:21-23)

Sarah, unhappy with Hagar's ungrateful behaviour and disrespect, started to be harsh with her. Hagar, too proud and sensitive, fled away. The Angel of the Lord met her in the desert, since He had been watching her all along, and asked where she was coming from and where she was going. Of course, she didn't know the answer to the latter so she told Him that she was fleeing from Sarah, her mistress.

The Angel simply told her: "Return to your mistress, and submit yourself under her hand... I will multiply your descendants exceedingly, so that they shall not be counted for multitude." (Gen. 16:9,10) That meant "get back in your place as a servant and I will bless you."

Many problems come from this kind of behaviour. People don't know their place in society, in marriage, in relationships, in their work place, and so forth. Hagar was a servant to a blessed couple and yet she forgot her place as a servant and tried by force to grab hold of a place that didn't belong to her, and that was when she gave birth to the problems we hear about today.

If only Hagar did what the Angel said and submitted to her mistress, Ishmael would have grown up to be a man of God as well, and surely not give birth to a generation of people full of grudges against their own brother's generation! If only Ishmael had been raised by Abraham and Sarah as their own son. If only...

A wise woman knows her place, be it at home or in church. She knows what is expected of her and she does it as a good servant to Her Master, Her Lord, and Her Saviour. She will serve Him through her husband, children, parents, home, work, others, and her own body.

When we know our place, we don't struggle so much because everything starts falling into place with time—God Himself makes sure of that. What is your place?

Notes

_____

_____

_____

_____

_____

_____

_____

The Jumping We Effortlessly Do

I don't know why we do this, but it has been proven that it is in our nature to jump to conclusions without all the evidence needed. We look at someone and we quickly judge that person by her clothes, her skin colour, the way she walks, and so many other things that we quickly pick up by just casting our eyes in her direction. And we are so hard to please—if her hair is not well done, we think she's careless but if her hair is well done, we think she's too proud of it; if she smiles at everyone, we think she's trying too hard, but if she doesn't smile at all, we think she's a snob. And our standards go on and on, never reaching an attainable point.

I am ashamed to say that I have been on both sides of this fence. I have been judged and I have judged others. When I judged and later found out that I was completely wrong about that person, I felt as if I was the worst friend anyone could ever have. My thoughts about that person had been evil, angry, and malicious and when I think of it, I feel ashamed of myself, especially because that person ended up being this amazing woman I now know. Back when all this jumping to conclusions occurred, I thought she was this empty woman trying to be someone she was "obviously" not. A few years later, I came to know her better and I realised I had judged her totally wrong. She didn't know but God did and He saw how impure my eyes were towards her. If I could, I'd undo all those useless thoughts I let into my mind.

Then I found myself being judged—quite a few times actually. And it felt so unfair. I wanted to prove people wrong, I wanted to say something, but how could I? There was a time I wanted to prove them wrong so badly that I just could not rest until I did. I started to try too hard, doing anything and everything to make those people see that I wasn't what they thought I was. But nothing I did or said changed anything until I grew up spiritually and realised that I shouldn't waste my time and life trying to prove to people that they're wrong about me, that I would never ever please everyone, and that I would always come short of everybody's expectations— after all, I'm human! Sometimes people forget that we humans are supposed to make mistakes.

We'll never be good enough for people and that is okay, because we don't need to be good enough for them. God has chosen us this way, full of mistakes and shortcomings, He knew about all our weaknesses and still chose us from the midst of so many other women in this world who are probably more educated, more successful, and more everything. He didn't choose them but He did choose you and me. Can anyone ask more than be selected from among millions and millions of others just to make a difference in this world by their faith?

You—yes...you reader have been chosen by God to be an amazing woman in this world, despite all you've been or done. Don't lose this prize trying to impress people who aren't really going to make any difference in your life, instead, impress the only One who is worthy! Give Him your best and your all and wait and see His justice served in your life.

Notes

_____

_____

_____

_____

_____

_____

_____

_____

Who am I?

That's the question. But how can one live fully with that question in mind all the time? It is such a waste to see women with potential always asking this question, not knowing who they really are and who they should be. They live in this fantasy world where dreams can only happen whilst they're sleeping or daydreaming. Life for them is almost like a burden.

The world takes advantage of this need by offering them so many alternatives to reality. "Here, watch this soap opera and see how people out there also have their problems"—when soaps are directed by someone's imagination, and always end the way people would love it to end; or "Take a break and enjoy a trip to the Caribbean", but you and I know that though trips can be relaxing for a while, they don't solve the problem. You have to come home eventually and what then? or "Why not a makeover and become a totally new woman today?" But how can a makeover change what's unpleasant underneath?

It's a fact that nothing in this world can fill the gap that everyone has deep inside of them. No money, person, power, or status can actually make you complete. There will always be a question underneath: "What was I born for?" or "Why am I here?"

Look outside and see beyond what is going on around you. Look at the greatness of the skies, the miracle of a newborn baby, the immensity of the sea, the animals' amazing ability of caring for themselves, and nature's unfailing schedule. How could all this be without Someone actually designing it? How can anyone think that a random molecule one day could have created all that we see today. You've got to have more faith to believe that than to believe the obvious—that there is a God!

As long as you try to live your life without truly pursuing the reason why you were created, you'll never be happy—no matter how rich or famous you become, or whether you have a family or not. Happiness is only possible when one can find the answer to this question that is common to every human.

Before having had an encounter with my Creator, I used to question so many things in life. I wondered why I was here and how everything I saw began. I knew the answer was right in front of me but I just couldn't see it. I knew there was a God, after all I had been taught about Him all my life, but I didn't really know Him personally. A lot of people go through the same problem throughout the world today.

People hear and learn about God but still live wondering about so much. It's not enough just to know about Him, because that doesn't fill the gap inside of us. It was only when I met Him personally that I was filled and never was the same again. I found happiness right there. I became certain of who I was and where I was going. I knew where I was coming from and why I was here. Everything made sense for me and I felt complete.

Who are you? Know God personally in your life and you won't wonder about that anymore.

Notes

_____

_____

_____

_____

_____

_____

_____

_____

_____

_____

Mirror, Mirror

As you wake up in the morning, one of the first things you do is look in the mirror. Sometimes, it's to remember your face and sometimes it's just to wonder who that person looking back at you is really up to—no make-up, hair all messed up, tired and baggy eyes with a big question mark. You wonder if the way you look has anything to do with the way your marriage is changing or why you just can't attract the right man. And those harsh comments a guy made or painful remarks a friend made about the way you look start storming into your mind—are they true? "Am I not good enough? What's wrong with me?" You ask, clueless.

Why would something be wrong with you? Have you ever thought that perhaps the reason the mirror is giving you is something else entirely? People say that inner beauty is what matters, but how come so many women are extremely gentle and good in their character, and yet so sad and discontented? What is your mirror actually trying to say to you?

One can't help but realise that inner beauty is not enough to make a woman look in the mirror and love what she sees. Neither is appearance, because there are plenty of extremely beautiful women who hate what they see in their mirror as well, and so many turn to drugs or whatever can make them forget their clueless life. You may even have a family of your own, a husband who adores you, a house you own, and the perfect job—yet you still don't have what it takes and the mirror is still trying to tell you something.

More often than not, we need to go to the source, the beginning of things, in order to find why things are the way they are. One day, thousands of years ago, the first woman was created. Eve lived in Paradise and she had everything. She was happy and fulfilled in every way and God's plan for her was to multiply by giving birth to many other women who would be just as happy. Nevertheless, Eve decided to walk on her own, and with that she forsook Her Creator, True Father, and Best Friend.

From then on, women have been born clueless of how special they were meant to be. And why? Because they don't realise that they'll only be fulfilled when they look for the One True Boyfriend, Best Friend, Father, Husband, and Heart's Treasure! They keep going round and round, seeking for "Mr. Right" when in fact, the only way to find him is through their faith. Wives keep on praying and fighting for their husbands to become one thing or another, whilst change can only happen through their relationship with God.

Psalm 90:17 says, "... Let the beauty of the Lord our God be upon us..." That's what mirrors are trying to say whenever you look at them and wonder how else can you beautify yourself. You need God, but not just as any god in this world—you need Him more than you need a husband, a boyfriend, a friend, a child, and life itself.

To have God is not just to believe in Him, but also to have a true, deep relationship with Him. And you know when you have this because every time you look in the mirror, you're as happy as you can be—even when there's no one else or nothing else in your life to cling on to.

So to answer your question—there's nothing wrong with you. You just need to know your Creator, and you'll have everything you need to have a fulfilled life!

Notes

_____

_____

_____

_____

_____

_____

Template Girl

It's so typical for girls to want to look like other popular girls, to dress the way they do, and have the friends they have, and even speak like them. Some go to the extent of being rude like them—parents usually are the first to suffer that kind of treatment. Thankfully, they grow up and become mature enough to be their own selves. They dress the way they like to and are friends with those they feel good with.

And then they meet God for the first time in their life and everything changes. All they want is to please Him and serve Him. Some practically live in the church, always so active in church groups and activities. They even neglect their quality time at home.

However—yes, there we go again—things start changing; they start looking around and behaving just like other young women in the church. They look at the assistants and the pastor's wife and they immediately go back to the old days and decide it's time to look like someone else. And that is how we get actresses of God. But, I ask, and please don't be mad at me, why? Why be someone you're not? Why be like everyone else?

All of a sudden, you're not yourself anymore but a completely different person. Some may think they just matured, but I say, they're not being who they are.

When you become a true Christian, you change from feeling, thinking, and doing the wrong things. That's all! You don't change your personality; instead, you open up even more. You become your best self. Your mind opens up to understand the things that really matter and you mature spiritually as time goes by.

The process is similar to that of a diamond. When it's found, it's rough and ugly and may look like any other common stone, but when it's cleaned, cut, and polished, it becomes "a girl's best friend"! Beautiful, sparkling, brilliant—one of a kind. This is exactly what God does to us. Before having an encounter with Him, we're confused, not knowing exactly where we're going or what we're doing with our life. We look like everybody else in the world, completely lost and incapable of taking control in life. We feel as if we're playing some kind of game, in which the rules are completely unknown to us. And we lose every time.

It is only on the day of our new birth that we start seeing things in a different way. We're cleaned, cut, and polished in such a way that all the wrong things we've done in the past just don't matter anymore. We evolve into a real beauty from the inside out, different from everyone else in this world—holy, one of a kind!

Let us then be who we are, different, unique, and special in our own ways, not following the crowd, not trying to be like so and so, but being the best we can be. Be the short red-haired woman or the tall young woman in red—whoever you are or however you look, be proud of it because you know what? Your Lord chose you just like that! Hey, that has got to mean something.

Notes

_____

_____

_____

_____

_____

_____

_____

_____

_____

_____

_____

The Self-Help Method

There are times when we feel so insecure about our lives, it seems as though everything is against us, draining all our inner strength.

We feel alone and misunderstood by even those closest to us and the thought of disappearing is appealing. We begin to ask why, but the answer is not forthcoming. Then we wonder why the faith we used so powerfully yesterday is not around to help us beat today's "blues".

When we pray, words seem too simple to explain how we feel inside and we can't help but groan hoping that God can comprehend our deepest feelings. People may try to understand, but it's unexplainable and if we try to explain, we feel foolish in doing so for words can't really describe our feelings.

Every woman goes through these hard times. You may be full of the Holy Spirit, but if you are human (which I believe you are), from time to time you will pass through these distressing moments.

This brings to mind a verse in Ecclesiastes, *"It is better to go to the house of mourning than to go to the house of feasting... Sorrow is better than laughter; for by the sadness of the countenance the heart is made glad."* (Eccl. 7:2,3)

When we feel sad and lonely, that's when we give God a chance to work in us. For instance, have you ever had a cheerful heart while repenting of something wrong you've done? Of course not, that is impossible.

When we repent, we feel truly sorry for what we have done, and with that true sorrow, we feel ashamed, which leads us to the decision—never to do it again.

In these distressing times, wallowing in self-pity and cowering in an isolated corner, hoping that these things will pass away and return to normal, is of no use at all. Instead, we must use the best self-help method that has proven to be effective throughout the centuries—prayer.

Prayer is the ability to communicate with the only One who can truly help us in hard times. It has worked in the lives of millions, both in the past and present, worldwide. It has worked and is working in my life.

When I pray, I like to think that I am a little girl speaking to my father. I don't have to sound mature. I just express what I feel inside, unconcerned if my words are pronounced correctly or if I am saying the right thing. Before God I am myself, which seems to be enough for Him. I feel at ease, and can say whatever comes to mind because I know He understands me fully.

While others can't read my heart, He can and that is why I tell Him things I would never tell anyone else.

Women lose so much in this aspect. We usually like to speak our minds to our friends thinking that they understand us, but do they really? Most men I know find it so difficult to understand women, and we can't understand ourselves either. But God does. He understands us because He is the One who created us.

God knows you inside out. He understands why you behave the way you do and He wants you to know that He can help if you only talk to Him from the bottom of your heart. Don't worry if you don't know how to pray, prayer doesn't require knowledge at all. It only requires sincerity and faith.

If you are praying from the bottom of your heart and you believe that God is listening to your prayer, then that is all you need to know—that He is right there beside you. And if you are going through hard times, He is even closer to you. God is close to the broken-hearted because that is when we seek Him most. And as the previous verse mentioned, "...by the sadness of the countenance, the heart is made glad."

During this amazing experience of talking with our Creator, we desire just to freeze time and stay in His presence forever. It's interesting how easily we forget this feeling when we're busy and the temptation of just "thinking" a simple prayer comes to our mind.

We think that we can't take time to talk to God, that we've got things to do and places to go; that there is just not enough time to pray. That's why we are driven to hard times and tribulations in our lives, so that soon enough, we remember to pray. It's unfortunate, but true that when we are happy we tend to distance ourselves from God.

We so easily forget His presence in our lives and tend to give our time to things that bring us nothing in the end. We are so stubborn but even so, God understands us and is ready to give us a helping hand when we reach out to Him.

Prayer helps depression, suicidal thoughts, insecurity, emptiness, disappointment, loss of a loved one, anger, anxiety, stress, and the list goes on. Do you know any other self-help method more effective than this?

Notes

_____

_____

_____

_____

_____

_____

_____

_____

_____

_____

_____

_____

All the Beauty in the World

Many of us would like to look as beautiful as the celebrities often seen in movies and magazines. They always seem to have the perfect face, skin, and body. Their lives are full of glamour—travelling around the world, endless parties, being admired by everyone, and having the money to buy whatever they want.

But this apparent "beauty" we see in them is merely part of the public persona they display. We can't comment on their real lives; it would be unfair since we don't know them personally, but we can certainly see (taking into account the many failed relationships, suicide attempts, drug and alcohol dependencies, etc.) that their lives are far from perfect.

In reality, their beauty is an outward quality that fades with time. Soon the news about today's celebrities are quickly replaced with stories about rising young stars. If we want to have all the beauty in the world, we need to stop looking for it in the wrong places.

What's the secret?

We should and must take good care of our appearance, but our main concern should be how to attain and keep the true beauty that only God can give. A woman of God has much beauty. She does not need any make-up or special creams to enhance it—her presence is enough.

Her sincere smile makes you want to know her "secret".

She has a gentle quality when she speaks that one could almost call angelic. Her clothes are neither glamorous nor glitzy, and yet the whole room shines when she enters. She may not be famous, but people who meet her desire to be like her.

She may be young and inexperienced, but her qualities reveal to others her care and love as a mother. Her children want to grow up and be like her or marry someone just like her. Her husband is proud to have her as his wife and enjoys being in her company. Her friends are curious about what makes her so different.

Why is she so different from everyone else? It's because she has met the Author of all beauty. When a woman meets God, she becomes just like Him and through her, all her family and friends can be blessed. She becomes a light and wherever she goes, her light dispels any surrounding darkness. This makes her the most beautiful woman in the world.

If we want to become a woman of God and have an encounter with Him, we must first remove all the things that can impede Him from coming inside us. God is Perfect, Holy, Pure, Good, and much more.

In order for us to meet Him, we must remove everything that is contrary to His nature such as: impure thoughts, envy, jealousy, lies, dirty talk, gossip, evil intentions, and all things that can make one's conscience unclean.

When all these things have been removed, only then will we be ready for God to reveal Himself to us. The past and all the bad things that ever happened in our lives will be completely erased as if they had never happened—and we will become totally new women.

This is the most amazing experience a person could ever wish for. After an encounter with God, we wake up each morning and look forward to the new day ahead. Disappointments and problems no longer put us down because the strength within us carries us on for better things to come.

Notes

Cherish

*I*t is unfortunate but true that many people come to Jesus almost crawling their way in, and when they are cleansed, fed, dressed, and taught a better way to live, they quickly forget where they came from and start complaining that things are not quite as they expected.

This is the reason why the blessings God already promised are so delayed. He wants to continue showering us with His blessings, but how can He if we are always complaining, losing heart, doubting, and on the verge of giving up?

It is so easy to forget what we've conquered so far and extremely easy to remember the things that are still on hold in our lives. A woman who does not cherish the blessings she has so far will have a hard time seeing more come her way.

Why not cherish the love you found when you met the Lord Jesus? Can you remember anyone loving you as much? Why not cherish the peace you have now when you place your head on your pillow? Remember those sleepless nights?

Have you ever felt higher than when you are sensing the presence of God? Have you ever had so much assurance of where you're going? Just look around your life and see how much has changed so far, and cherish these changes. They wouldn't be around if it weren't for your coming to know the Lord Jesus.

Whenever you feel down and discouraged by something you heard or saw, remember that God is right there beside you and He knows everything that is going on in your life, even sad news or horrible disappointments. He knows and He will take care of you; just cherish Him always—don't become dismayed.

One of the most valuable teachings I received from my father was that my faith is the most precious thing I have and I should never let anything or anyone take it away from me. Till this day, I remember this teaching and keep it within my heart.

I know there are times that make us confused and even ungrateful to God, but you know what? These are the times He is closest to us! Sometimes, the best thing to do when you're feeling this way is to go to bed early and wake up the next day with a refreshed mind and spirit. In other words, sleep on it!

Cherish your husband if you have one—many women only wish they had one by their side right now. Cherish your child—soon he'll grow up and be gone from under your wings and you'll miss him dearly. Cherish your family—they may be full of faults, but deep down, they love you and just can't find a better way to express their love.

Cherish the times you come to church—many are those who wish they had one in their hometown. Cherish your work—be excellent at it and soon you'll be cherished there as well. Cherish your home—give it your time; don't treat it like a hotel because it's the special place meant for you to have private, quality time. Cherish your life—it was bought at a very high price, our Lord Jesus' life.

Notes

_____

_____

_____

_____

_____

_____

_____

_____

Eve's Mistakes

'How long, you simple ones, will you love simplicity?' (Pv. 1:22)

Many times we fail in our trials as mother, wife, and even as a friend—and we don't even know why. We blame everybody and everything, and sometimes even God.

Let's look at women of God. Why do they inspire us? What is the secret of these women we meet throughout the Bible and even come across in our personal lives? What do they have that makes them so cherished and honoured?

God made us women with a great power to either lift a man up high or push him down into the deepest pit. When we consider Eve, we see an example of this power in action when she influenced her husband to deliberately disobey the Creator, which consequently brought sin into the world. Since then, there have been women, and there have been women—those who inspire and those who shame. Let's meditate on Eve's life and see what it is that makes us capable of causing so much trouble.

Eve was God's last creation. She must have been stunningly beautiful. Upon her existence, she found a paradise beyond imagination, plus a perfect man who adored her. Eve was as happy as a woman could be—no bad memories, no past, no tears of disappointment, no diseases or pain, and no lack for anything she could possibly need. All she did in life was live it to the full by her husband's side.

One day, during one of her walks alone in the garden, the serpent approached her very subtly and enticed her to believe in a lie. At first, she denied the serpent, standing firm on what she knew was right; but then as soon as the serpent offered her the opportunity to gain knowledge of things unknown, she quickly gave in to its suggestion and ate of the forbidden fruit. Eve believed in that serpent, not because she was evil or wanted to go against God, but solely because she was a simple and naïve woman who just thought she could better herself. And with her naïveté, she enticed her husband to do the same, thinking that she was doing him a favour.

That was it for Eve; in one simple misunderstanding, she brought all that was evil upon herself, upon her husband, her children, and every living thing in existence. The Bible says, *"Only simpletons believe everything they are told! The prudent carefully consider their steps."* (Pv. 14:15). In other words, a woman may be of God, but if she is simple she can be used by the devil just the same as the devil's own people. With her words and attitudes, she can cause separation in her own family, trauma to her own children, disgust to her own husband, and bad memories to her own friends. God says, *"How long, you simple ones, will you love simplicity?"* (Pv. 1:22)

Wisdom is to know how to speak and deal with people around us. Wisdom can be found if we just seek it wholeheartedly, as promised by God in the book of Proverbs. Many women think they know better, which is why they never attain it because only those who feel the need for wisdom are able to find it. If you humbly ask God for His wisdom in your life and seek it with all your heart, if you are prepared to adjust your whole way of life, no matter your background or culture, God will gladly give it to you, and you too will be a woman who inspires others and is honoured by all those who have the privilege of knowing you.

Our ability to change a man's life is clearly shown when the apostle Peter exhorts, *"Wives, likewise, be submissive to your own husbands, that even if some do not obey the word, they, without a word, may be won by the conduct of their wives, when they observe your chaste conduct accompanied by fear."* (1 Pe. 3:1,2) Can you imagine how powerful that is?

It is even more interesting to see that God does not mention such ability with men; we may be the "weaker vessel", but a truly vital one indeed.

Notes

Attitude Problem—Me?

*O*nce upon a time there was a woman who, for some reason, was avoided by everyone who knew her. There were nights that she cried herself to sleep, asking God what was wrong with her. She had always heard how good it was to have friends, but had never actually had even one. One day, she finally got the nerve to ask another woman what she thought of her. And that was when she was told very carefully that she had an attitude problem.

An attitude problem usually consists of things you say and do that hurt others. You may have a valid reason to be upset, and yet your attitude towards the situation will actually steal your reason and make you become the problem. Many people hardly ever realise they have this problem, because they usually think their angry words and actions were necessary in order to make a point.

The problem is that you can never rationally make a point when you have lost your temper. People just can't see your point—they can't hear what you're saying, just how you're saying it and the way you're acting. In other words, when you lose your temper with someone, you're actually making yourself the one at fault; instead of the person looking at her own mistakes, she'll only be looking at yours.

Besides that, you become disliked among those who know you, and even among those who could get to know you, but don't because of what they hear. They never know what will push your buttons, how you'll react, or when it's safe to come near you. It's almost as if you can turn yourself into "The Incredible Hulk" at anytime!

It's even worse to see this in a woman, who is supposed to be such a lovely and gentle being. Women who start an argument with the cashier or the salesperson are usually looked upon as problematic customers. You see, when we lose control of our sweetness, we also lose our beauty in an instant, becoming the problem itself. I'm sure you'll agree with me the minute you remember the last time you witnessed a woman lose her temper and start a scene in front of everyone. It's just a shame, even more, for those who call themselves "Christians".

You can tell when you have an attitude problem when you are constantly telling people off. If you don't like what you see or hear, you don't have to repeat it by telling people off, do you? Instead, calm down, count to 10 or 100, and let the moment pass. You can always take this to the next day, when you have thought properly about how to deal with it.

Women with an attitude problem have difficulties finding friends. They are very hard to be with and instead of getting the results they want or earning the respect of others, they get the opposite. It's all right to demand your rights, but never to use your rights to disrespect others.

The Bible says in Proverbs 27:15 that *"A continual dripping on a very rainy day and a contentious woman are alike."* How about that? The woman with an attitude problem is being compared to one of the most irritating noises in the world—the continual dripping of water. Who can tolerate that?

Notes

_____

_____

_____

_____

_____

_____

_____

_____

Had Enough of Yourself?

$\mathcal{S}$ometimes the only way to change a situation is when we conclude that we've had enough of it.

There are things in our lives that we tend to leave aside hoping they disappear by themselves. But instead, they sink their roots deeper and deeper with each year that passes until we think, "They're too deep to be pulled out. Better leave them as they are."

The "That's the way I am and people just have to get used to it" attitude can sometimes become a burden to others, as well as put up a strong barrier to block new friends.

I used to think this way until the day I learned that I could be whoever I wanted to be and do whatever I wanted to do. At first I struggled a lot and got quite embarrassed by doing things nobody ever saw me do, but I kept on with determination, and in due course, it got easier and easier until the day I didn't struggle with it anymore.

There is a time in everyone's life that some things have to give and some things have to change. That is when we say ENOUGH of a certain situation and break out of our norm to unleash the Power of Enough inside of us. I did it and it works!

God is constantly giving us opportunities to change, but it's really up to us to accept them. It's like a potted plant that needs pruning. If you don't prune it, it will grow too much and the pot will soon become too small, making it weak and eventually killing it.

Likewise, we need to be pruned from time to time. There are things in us that are just taking up space in our lives, things that don't let us grow or become better women, things that impede us from making a difference among our friends, relatives, and family.

The pruning itself hurts. For the plant, it makes it look ugly and lifeless. For us, it makes us blush and feel humiliated, but later on, like the plant that becomes fuller and more beautiful, we become better women whose example inspires other women.

God wants us to be like this lovely potted plant that decorates this world so beautifully, exhaling a nice fragrance, inspiring many other women, and making a big difference in an odd and crazy world. He wants us to be of use, but it is up to us to accept it or not.

We normally hide withered plants in a back room or even throw them away, but the beautiful ones are on display in the best rooms. Isn't that what happens to us as well? Women who are always giving up or causing problems tend to be left alone or put aside, but how pleasant it is to be among women who are constantly changing for the better.

Use the Power of Enough inside you and change yourself. Let the woman of God inside you live long and free because it is not about who you are, but what kind of woman God wants you to be. Get it? Had enough?

Notes

_____

_____

_____

_____

_____

_____

_____

_____

_____

_____

_____

_____

Rachel & Leah

*L*eah is rarely mentioned when women in the Bible are discussed, and yet she was a woman worthy of admiration. She went from rejection to humiliation and then to loneliness and yet despite all that, instead of turning against God, she turned to Him and became a woman of God.

Although the much talked about Rachel, her sister, appears first in the Bible, Leah's story begins when her father gives her into marriage by deceit to Jacob. She was the forsaken one of her household, and now, for the first time, she was going to be respected as Jacob's wife. Nevertheless, her joy lasted only for a night, and she was back to being the rejected and humiliated one when Jacob woke up and saw, in clear disappointment, that he'd married Leah instead of Rachel.

Rachel, her younger sister who owned Jacob's heart, came into the picture again and married Jacob, leaving Leah to be the spare wife. And so Leah began her relationship with God, whom she must have met through Jacob's living testimony. Contrary to her sister, she grew closer to God.

God saw Leah's situation and started to bless her by giving her children. Rachel, on the other hand, had good looks and Jacob's love, but she did not have the same faith and evidently was not blessed with children, *"...when Rachel saw that she bore Jacob no children, Rachel envied her sister, and said to Jacob, 'Give me children, or else I die!'"* And Jacob's anger was aroused against Rachel, and he said, *"Am I in the place of God, who has withheld from you the fruit of the womb?"* (Ge. 30:2)

Rachel had many reasons to be happy, apart from not having children. At least she was happily married to Jacob; but her jealousy blinded her from seeing that her sister was finally having a break in life. All she could think of was how her sister, Leah, was getting ahead of her and her perfect little world was becoming too small for both of them. She started to use her servant to sleep with Jacob, and in revolt, she named each child her servant bore, according to her spitefulness. One in particular showed Rachel's state of mind concerning her sister: *"Then Rachel said, 'With great wrestling I have wrestled with my sister, and indeed I have prevailed.' So she called his name Naphtali."* (Ge. 30:8)

It is interesting to note how different one was from the other. We see how grateful Leah was when God blessed her with children and how envious Rachel was. Just by the way she named "her" children, you can see her spiritual state! Rachel had the looks, the popularity, and the love of Jacob, but wasn't a woman of God. She had relied on all that to become the perfect wife but still, she was neither complete, nor felt complete. Leah didn't have the looks, was disregarded most of her life, was considered a mistake by Jacob, and yet she was a woman of God whose descendants include the Lord Jesus Himself.

A woman of God may go through the hardest times, but she will always keep her integrity. She is happy for those who are blessed and she trusts that God will bless her in time. Not once do we see Leah hate Rachel, but we definitely cannot say the same thing about Rachel.

Rachel didn't have the same faith of Jacob, after all, she had his heart already and that is why we see such a difference between her and her sister. Rachel lived to keep score, always looking at others and envying them, no matter how little there was to envy.

These kinds of women look at other women from top to bottom and sometimes will even judge them to be one thing or another, but the reality is that envy takes control of them and they just cannot stand the existence of women of God. They pray and fast but with their envious eyes they end up becoming cursed and incomplete. Those whom they reject become the ones honoured by the Lord Jesus—no matter their background, their looks, or their unpopularity.

"For where envy and self-seeking exist, confusion and every evil thing are there." (Jas. 3:16)

Notes

_____

_____

_____

Real Christians' Fear

"I can't do it! I can't practise the Word of God as much as I try, ...and worse, the more I try, the less I do it!" This was murmured once by a young lady from the youth group after hearing a strong message on a Wednesday. She was really sad, but at the same time, very defensive, as if it was too much for God to ask of us to practise His Word.

The problem is that when a woman does not fear God, she finds it very hard to do what He says. It's just like the parent/child relationship. The child, usually at a very young age, doesn't need to learn that she needs to respect and obey her parents. She learns that by all the discipline she goes through in her childhood. She obeys because, deep down, she knows that her parents know better. And so she naturally fears her parents.

An employee that fears her boss will also do what he or she tells her to do, even if she doesn't feel like doing so. She does it because she respects her boss, who is able to fire her at any time in case she doesn't. This employee fears her boss.

Many Christians, however, don't fear God. They often think of God as someone very lovely who would never, ever be angry with them, someone who is always ready to forgive no matter if He has to do it every single minute of that person's life. And so, these so-called Christians live as comfortably as they please, not caring a bit about what God says.

Of course, they go to church; they like doing this to relieve their conscience, but only their bodies go to church, not their spirit. Their minds stay at home, at work, with the children, with the relatives, on the football match, and so on. Their life is a totally different story from the life they pretend to have.

On Sunday mornings, they put on their best clothes to impress in church. They sit wherever is most convenient to leave as soon as the service is finished. As a matter of fact, they can't wait for the meeting to end because it's such a burden to be there. They try to get to church as late as possible; after all, they aren't that interested in the first part of the meeting anyway.

These "Christians" don't respect God in any way. They take the things of God lightly as if their salvation were a joke. Their mouths will more often than not say evil about others. Their eyes are constantly judging and envying others. Their minds are always full of worldly thoughts. Their feet walk towards the wrong crowd and their hands are nothing but tools in order to do evil.

Of course if they read this, they'll immediately feel accused and judged, but that's because they relate to this and God is warning them *"...do not fear those who kill the body but cannot kill the soul. But rather fear Him who is able to destroy both soul and body in hell."* (Mt. 10:28)

Notes

Say Cheese!

ℐt can be depressing to walk around nowadays. So many angry faces and "couldn't care less" expressions that make one wonder if it's still a good option to raise children. People everywhere, and yet so cold and indifferent to everybody else around.

Everybody talks about peace and how the world should be at peace, but how can the world be at peace if it's so hard to get a smile from someone in the street or even from a neighbour? People look at the big picture, but just can't seem to see the missing pieces for that picture to be made complete.

The problem is within people. It cannot be solved by peace agreements or peace conferences, or even peace rallies. It lies in the heart. A person who does not know God is empty and vain. Many people say they know God but how can they know Him and have such a sad face? Impossible!

When we know God, we may be going through problems yet still have a smile on our face. Our problems are only external and can be overcome by our faith. But when a woman does not know God, her problems start from within. She may even use her faith to overcome them, but she will still not be complete.

"A merry heart makes a cheerful countenance, but by sorrow of the heart the spirit is broken." (Pr. 15:13)

If you always find your spirit broken and have difficulty smiling, it's very likely that you still need to know God. Going to church does not mean that you know Him—it means that you hear about Him and that you are trying to get to know Him. But this encounter with Him will only happen when you realise your need to know Him.

Think of all of your problems for a moment: If all of them were solved, would you be happy? Would that be enough for your life to be complete? Can you remember when you didn't have these problems? Were you fulfilled then?

When we know God:

• We become so wise, capable of understanding things like no one else in this world. As 1 Corinthians 1:15,16 says, "But he who is spiritual judges all things, yet he himself is rightly judged by no one. For who has known the mind of the LORD that he may instruct Him? But we have the mind of Christ."

• We become His children; can you imagine being a child of the MOST HIGH? We think like He does. We behave like Him. We even look like Him. We find that it's extremely easy for us to smile. People look at us and even think that we have no problems! As 1 Corinthians 6:17 says, *"But he who is joined to the Lord is one spirit with Him."*

So what are you waiting for? Are you waiting to get a bit older and realise that you missed out on the best years of your life? Are you waiting to solve all your problems and realise that you'll never be fulfilled? Are you waiting to have more time and realise that time will never be enough?

Be wise and get to know God personally... and soon, you'll be saying "cheese" from the inside out!

Notes

_____

_____

_____

_____

_____

_____

_____

_____

Selfish Old Gal

Money, clothes, jewellery, house, car, and so on are things that constantly show what kind of person we are. It's not the way we dress, or the way we take care of these things that does it, but the importance we give to them. Sometimes a woman holds onto these things because she lacked them all her life and sometimes she does it because she just loves having more and more. For this reason, many women end up losing what little they have, going without, and even lacking more.

There's never enough for them. Life is never sufficient. They've got to have more of this, more of that, hold on to the little they have, and never, ever think of sharing any of it. Reading this may even make them feel annoyed, but if they really think about it, they're one of these women. When was the last time you gave something away? When was the last time you went without so that someone could have in your place—just for the pleasure of giving?

I learned this lesson when I was still very young. My mother always made sure she'd never miss an opportunity to give. We didn't have much ourselves, but every Christmas we'd give most of our toys to the children from the slums of Rio. We learned to let go of things early in life so that as we grew older, things would never, ever dictate what we were. I was only eight, but the pleasure of seeing those little children get my best doll just made the sacrifice worthwhile. We had never met and perhaps will never meet. Those children never knew why my family and I gave them those gifts. Nevertheless, we were the ones most blessed. The more we gave, the more God would give back to us.

I guess the problem is inside the person. She doesn't realise that the more she holds on to the little she has, the less she'll have. It's written and it's been proven. Look at people who are selfish. See if they're happy with what they have. I bet there's never enough and whatever they have never adds up. I have different types of friends—some who go out of their way to give and some who are only happy to receive. I usually give to both kinds but deep down I know the ones that are truly blessed. They may not be able to afford the world, but they surely can afford to go without in order to give and that is what makes the difference between one friend and another, one woman and another, one Christian and another.

Some are ready to sacrifice and others are only ready to receive. Who gets to receive at the end of the day? The ones who sacrificed! There's no but, there's no other way, there's no excuse to beat the fact that if you don't give, you don't receive. What else is there to explain? Why should anyone question it? Ask yourself when was the last time you gave and sacrificed for someone else, then answer that sincerely. Do you want any more proof as to why you're not being blessed?

Notes

_____

_____

_____

_____

_____

_____

_____

_____

_____

_____

_____

_____

Sensitive Girl

Sensitive:

1. Easily affected by something.

2. Easily offended or hurt.

3. Able to measure finely and exactly.

Some women look for sensitive guys, others are proud to say they're sensitive, and others still wish they were more sensitive. But if we look at the above description from the dictionary, we can conclude that being sensitive can be both positive and negative at the same time, which should immediately alert us.

We women, can be too sensitive sometimes, be it to a comment made or something that didn't turn out as we planned, or simply because it's one of those days of the month. It's alright to be sensitive to certain things in life, for instance, we need to be sensitive to our loved ones' needs. Sometimes they won't say it but they're in need of love, care, attention, and so forth. If we're not sensitive to their needs, we won't be doing enough, even if we try.

So sometimes, circumstances in life demand this from us, especially we women. Nevertheless, problems demand exactly the opposite. You can't overcome a problem by being sensitive. A problem is often a persistent thing that bothers us—it may be a disease, your teen's attitude problem, an addiction, etc. Whenever people deal with their problems with a sensitive heart, there's self-pity and that's one of the worst things about a sensitive person.

You feel sorry for yourself. You want others to feel sorry for you. And when that doesn't happen, you feel even more sorry for yourself because you're not being understood, people don't love you enough, you're not worthy, and the list of negative thoughts goes on and on. The next thing you know, you're nagging like that proverb in the Bible, "A continual dripping on a very rainy day and a contentious woman are alike." (Pr. 27:15)

Some of us women are pros at that. No wonder we feel alone—who can bear such attitude? Self-pity blinds us. It doesn't let us look at what is causing the problem and how we can deal with it. Instead, it makes us blame ourselves and others, which clearly does not solve the problem.

It's unfortunate to see how many women don't understand this. Women of all ages, young and old, simply don't realise they do wrong by being sensitive when the situation calls for the opposite: being insensitive, tough, hard-nosed, and so forth. Weakness, mistakes, injustice, and problems require a tough attitude. You need to be strong, not look for anyone's sympathy, and be in the faith.

How can faith be used with self-pity or sensitivity? Impossible! A woman who bled for 12 years heard about the Lord Jesus' miracles and believed. She didn't care that she was going to travel under the hot sun with all those cloths wrapped around her waist; all she cared about was to be healed. She said: "If only I may touch His clothes, I shall be made well" (Mk. 5:28). Some of us today would have stayed home and waited for a visit, and if that didn't happen, we'd call in and complain to the bishop. When the woman touched the Lord Jesus' clothes, she was immediately healed. Notice that she didn't demand a special appointment for that; she didn't make a big scene when people were pushing here and there to see Jesus, and she didn't even demand His attention. This woman used her intelligent faith. She was tired of the 12 years of being an unfair victim of a disease. But she decided to be insensitive to that and so she was able to use her faith and be healed. What about you? How long will you feel sorry for yourself?

Notes

_____

_____

_____

_____

Snow

I was 12 years old when I first saw snow. My family and I took loads of pictures and it seemed like heaven to us. Coming from a country where snow is only seen in the movies, you can imagine how happy we were to feel it in our hands! I can still remember today how it felt and looked. Whilst my family played and talked about it, I suddenly stopped and stared at its whiteness. My eyes hurt and I immediately remembered the song we used to sing in church "whiter than the snow".

To think that we're whiter than the snow every time we are forgiven by God should kill all the other evil thoughts about the past in our minds. We suffer a lot because we just won't take the things of God as the simple facts they are. God is not complicated, as a matter of fact, He couldn't be simpler. In Isaiah 1:18, He says, *"Come now, and let us reason together, though your sins are like scarlet, they shall be as white as snow; though they are red like crimson, they shall be as wool."*

Even so, people still try to hold on to the very things that tie them down to their misery, their past. They can't accept themselves and can't believe that God, being

Almighty, will! They have been given everything they could possibly need for a life they always dreamed. But still they think they're not worth all those blessings, and so they keep their insecurities locked up inside their hearts. And what for? Only just because they think they can never be as white as snow. If you bought a product and wanted to find out how it worked, you'd first read the manual, obviously. So then, let's do just that.

Read the following as a manual with instructions on how to start your life again. If you have repented from your past, that is, you've decided to leave your past behind because you don't want to make the same mistakes again, and would like God's help for that, follow these instructions and make sure you don't add or remove anything:

1. Ask God for forgiveness. No need to memorise words from any book, just say to God what you feel inside—exactly how you feel it. You don't need to put it in writing, just speak to Him and that will be fine.

2. Believe that He has forgiven you. He promised to and there's no reason why He wouldn't fulfil His promise, no matter how many mistakes you've made or how bad they were. His forgiveness is unconditional, so enjoy the privilege!

3. Leave it in the past and move on by faith. Like God, you must now also leave your past where it belongs and move on. This time however, do it right and move on with God.

Once you follow these three steps, you're headed for a new beginning.

Notes

_____

_____

_____

_____

_____

_____

_____

_____

_____

_____

_____

_____

The Female Parasite

They can be very nice women, lovely in some ways, and they hardly ever give others problems because they have the habit of keeping to themselves. Life can be too dangerous for them to risk their time trying new things, so they stick to what's safe and secure. Inasmuch as they're nice women, they hardly make any difference in other peoples' lives.

The world is basically infested by such "nice" women and that is because most people don't really want to add or make any difference in the world. They'd be happy if they could get through their own lives, which is fair, acceptable—but sad. Sad because not only are they one more creature breathing our limited oxygen supply, but mostly because they are women who don't give—they're fruitless!

All the nice things we have access to today are due to people that were the complete opposite. People who decided one day to make a difference in the world. Though they knew they wouldn't ever be able to do it alone, they didn't use that excuse to keep them from doing something extraordinary, unexpected, which later on made such a difference.

"No one, when he has lit a lamp, covers it with a vessel or puts it under a bed, but sets it on a lamp stand, that those who enter may see the light." (Lk. 8:16)

Why would women who have met God and received His Spirit and direction be any less? If we have the light inside us, shouldn't it enlighten everyone and everything around us? Isn't it reasonable to think we must shine in this world? Why is it so hard to see this happening then? Why are there so few women who truly make a difference in this world?

Everything falls on those who are out there working on making a difference. They end up having to do it all and more (you know, the part that should have been shared by others). Like my father always says, a handful of people pushing a big overloaded truck of people on top of it. Parasites, people who live to enjoy the hard work and effort of others. Lovely, very nice, good people that make no difference in the world.

Employees that only work for the salary at the end of the month; colleagues that only do what they're told; children that only work towards their own future; mothers that live entirely for their children; wives whose only concern in life is to be happily married; assistants who love the fact that they have a uniform to wear and a position in the church; and pastors' wives who are just there to decorate the church—these are just a few examples of female parasites.

What about you? Are you a parasite, too? If you truly want to answer this question, consider how many times you've made a difference in the world. Don't count the times you were asked to—those times don't count. Parasites are asked to make a difference because they have to be told what to do.

A woman who makes a difference never needs anyone to tell her what to do because her entire being is always in search of what and where she can do more. She's a sign of God in this world.

Notes

_____

_____

_____

_____

_____

_____

_____

_____

_____

The Foreign Woman

This woman from Canaan heard about the Lord Jesus and the miracles He was performing everywhere He went. What she heard made her sure that He was the One who was going to put an end to her daughter's suffering. She then started going after Him, pleading for her daughter.

The disciples were getting tired of her insistence in getting the help she needed, and the Lord Jesus, knowing she was only after His miracle, ignored her for a time. Even then, she didn't stop asking for help. She must have annoyed everyone around her.

Knowing that this foreign woman wasn't going to stop pleading after Him, the Lord Jesus turned around and said: "It is not good to take the children's bread and throw it to the little dogs." By this time, people must have thought, "After this complete tell off, she'll definitely stop!"

But she said: "Yes, Lord, yet even the little dogs eat the crumbs which fall from their masters' table." The Lord Jesus was amazed at her answer; I mean, her attitude towards what He said was completely the opposite of what anyone would expect. So He said, *"O woman, great is your faith! Let it be to you as you desire."* (Mt. 15:22-28)

One of the most outstanding characteristics of this woman's faith is something called "humbleness". She was able to place herself where she belonged, not caring about her own ego and pride, even though the Lord Jesus told her off right there in front of everyone. This woman's faith is the kind of faith that many Christian women lack nowadays.

This is the kind of faith that is not put off by any little misunderstanding or scandal here and there. After all, she knows that her worth is due to the presence of her Lord in her life. Many women in this foreign woman's shoes would have marched off, furious at Jesus. Others would have started an argument with Him, and others still would have decided there and then to never, ever want to hear about Him again.

What kind of woman are you? What could actually push your buttons and drive you away from God? If you can think of something that might, you're not worthy of having God anyway. He's not the One who needs us but we desperately need Him. He's not the One at fault here—we're the ones. That woman knew that she didn't deserve anything from the Lord Almighty, and for that reason, she humbled herself and recognised her condition before God.

Some may think that the Lord Jesus here was quite rude, but if you think clearly, you'll see that He was right. She wasn't a believer and was probably there just to get her blessing, but the beautiful thing about it is that she recognised that and that's what many people lack.

The great wonders from God can only come upon the humble at heart. Little miracles here and there still can be achieved by a simple faith in Him, but great miracles can only be experienced when your faith is as great as this woman's: a faith that knows exactly where you stand before God.

Notes

_____

_____

_____

_____

_____

_____

_____

_____

_____

The Mask

There is a flaw that is apparent every now and then in some women. They seem to be so nice and friendly; sometimes you even feel inferior to them because of how they treat everybody around. And to your great shock, they end up being someone else completely different, and it's hard to really understand all the pretence.

Some people say many things just to please. They behave this or that way just to hide who they really are. But why? Why hide behind someone you're not? Isn't being yourself good enough for people? If not, then nobody is good enough for anyone because the last time I checked, we're all still humans, liable to commit mistakes.

How can we really know someone, if all they show is their good side and mask their real selves? How can anyone love someone who is not real? How can any friendship or relationship last this way?

The truth of the matter is that pretending to be someone you're not is actually a hard task. You have to keep up with all the lies you've said and always change the different masks—it's a hard job. And when your real self is exposed, you have to shamefully face the people whom you deceived. You have to think of excuses that won't make you look so bad and then there's the trust you lose with all the shame and humiliation.

Nobody was ever successful in being someone they weren't. They always show their true self sooner or later. Eventually everyone who lives this way is bound to be discovered and be known as a deceiver for the rest of their lives. People won't care about all the excuses they produce. All they'll care about is that they were lied to. And the deceiver will have made it harder for herself to be liked as a friend, wife, or a loved one.

So you see, being someone you're not is not easy at all! As long as you are yourself, people will love you for who you are with all your mistakes and flaws—and that's true love. They'll never have unrealistic expectations from you because they know you. And you can live in peace with yourself, never having to spend your time with masks or foolish reasons why you couldn't do something.

If you're exactly the person you are inside, you have a big chance of finding true love, true friendship, and most of all God—who by the way, knows you from inside out and will never accept masks and deceit. It just doesn't make sense, does it? You know the person and the person tries to show you she's someone else—it's just absurd. That's exactly how God feels and this may be the reason why many religious people in the world never really meet God personally.

Notes

_____

_____

_____

_____

_____

_____

_____

_____

_____

_____

_____

_____

_____

The Secret

A young lady who has been in the church for many years came to talk to me the other day. Her eyes were revealing a sadness I could not understand, after all, she was one of the most active women in the church, always making herself available to serve no matter the time, the place, or the person. I had always admired her faithfulness and good reputation before others, but now, there was something strange about her. As she opened up to me, a very deep secret was revealed: she had never really met the Lord she has been serving all her life.

Unfortunately, there are so many faithful people in the church who are in this situation. They have seen God's power in their lives, experienced some of God's promises, and yet have never really met Him personally. How can one serve or please Someone they don't know? They can't! They try for a time, but sooner or later, they feel exhausted in their faith, as if they were tired of doing good with no return whatsoever. Their spirit is dry and empty, their mind is full of question marks, their service to God gets tiresome, and so they wonder if He is really around.

God is always around, no question about that. The problem is that only those who truly know Him can actually see Him. They have an assurance He gives that He's there with them. Therefore they don't fear, don't give up, and don't despair when things get tough. Problems will always come, that is a fact, but overcoming them is guaranteed only by those who have met God personally, as the Bible says: *"For whatever is born of God overcomes the world: and this is the victory that overcomes the world, even our faith."* (1 Jo. 5:4)

So what now? You've discovered that the reason behind all your spiritual struggles is this lack of the new birth and you want to have it. But how? What are the conditions for one to be born of God or have an encounter with God?

The answer to these questions is: faith. Faith is the only way to God and the only way to conquer anything from Him. Simple as it is, people complicate this first step. They seem to believe that they have to be a certain way or that they should have never done what they did in the past, and now they are doomed to never, ever be born of God.

One thing is certain; you do not have to be perfect to be born of God. Nobody is perfect and God is not unfair to demand something that nobody on earth can be. However, you have got to stop doing the things you know are wrong before God. There are weaknesses, evil thoughts and doubts that you let in that are completely destructive to your faith. Sometimes a simple evil thought about yourself is the very reason why you have had difficulty in finding God because with these evil thoughts, faith cannot work, and if, your faith doesn't work, you cannot get to God.

Stop questioning God and the things of God. Stop complicating matters and leaving your faith behind. Faith is to believe in something you cannot yet see—that's all! If you believe, you will be born of God.

Notes

_____

_____

_____

_____

_____

_____

_____

_____

True Priorities

There is a huge flaw in many Christians nowadays. They live everyday as if there were no tomorrow, looking at their own interests and how to get a better life with all that God's promises can give. They fight and struggle to get a better job, a husband, a family, a business and a healing, but the one part of their life that will last forever is just never important enough to strive for: their spiritual life.

It's not wrong to pursue blessings, after all, the Lord Jesus did give us the right to be healthy, happy, and fulfilled. However, these shouldn't be the priorities of someone who knows about the things that are eternal and the things that are in a way, temporary.

What good is it for a woman to finally find a husband and then not have the strength within her to keep her marriage going strong? What good is it for a sick person to be healed but still be sick spiritually? How can a husband come back if all he's going to find is the same woman he couldn't stand for years? How can a relative want to know the Lord Jesus if the only one he could look up to as an example of the Lord Jesus lives an empty life?

Our spiritual life determines everything else in our life. If I am born of God, I will overcome in everything I intend to do, but if I am not born of God, I will struggle to have everything and will never be satisfied, because the one thing I need the most to hold onto all the blessings I conquer, I don't have—GOD inside of me.

People hear about the new birth all the time, and if they don't have it, it's not because they don't want it, but probably because they just don't make it a priority in their lives. The wise woman knows how to prioritise her life, as the definition says: "to order things according to their importance or urgency; to regard something as most important or urgent."

What is the most important thing a woman can have? Isn't it her own life? That should be her priority, before marriage, children, job, family, and even her health! It doesn't make sense to prioritise anything else if you don't have a strong inner self—a spiritual life.

Husbands leave, children disappoint, jobs are lost, money is spent, health is always at risk, and dreams will always exist—but our spirit will live eternally, either in peace or in torment. Shouldn't that be a future worth taking care of?

The world sometimes blinds us from seeing the real things in life. It offers all sorts of entertainment and pleasures beyond our needs, and at times we can even feel dizzy with its bright colours and attractions. It's all an illusion—every movie you watch, every song you listen to, every actor you applaud, behind the cameras and the heavy make-up all too often lies a soul who is lost, an empty spirit, and completely ignorant of what life is all about.

What do you prefer—to be successful for a couple of years or for all eternity? It's your call!

Notes

_____

_____

_____

_____

_____

_____

_____

_____

_____

_____

Wedding Feast

𝒯here was a king who was very eager to celebrate his son's wedding, but was turned down badly by the many cancellations by his VIP guests. So he decided to invite everyone in, the poor and the commoners of his kingdom. And so a multitude of people attended the wedding feast. But to the king's surprise, one of the guests was not dressed accordingly... the least the poor commoner could have done in order to participate in his party was to dress appropriately for the event! That was too much for the king to bear, so he immediately told his guards to throw this guest out in the street where *"there will be weeping and gnashing of teeth."* (Mt. 22:1-13)

The Lord Jesus told us this parable in order to illustrate the Kingdom of God. He came for those who were supposed to be His, but they rejected Him and so He extended His invitation to all of us Gentiles, poor, needy, lonely, and suffering. We accepted it wholeheartedly; after all, we had nothing to lose and had so much to gain.

Unfortunately, some of us take God's Kingdom for granted thinking that there's still a life and a future ahead without God's interference. And so, we don't bother to dress appropriately for His coming. We live life according to what others think is best and appropriate in today's world; worried about having as much fun as possible, without any commitment to hold onto in life. Our prospect of life is about ourselves and what the future will bring upon us. It's all about us and what our heart desires.

Completely unconcerned about how we're presenting ourselves to God, we live life as it comes. Bit by bit, struggle after struggle, we insist on not learning our lesson about life. We want to do it alone. Never mind that it's not God's will for us to go after our own hearts, after all, we're still young and free to do whatever we feel like doing. Independent from our parents and from anything or anyone in the world, we only worry about settling down when fun is no longer a need in our lives.

So undeserving and so stubborn, how can God deal with people like this? People who know what is right and what is not, and still insist on doing what is wrong? He tried to teach, and even now, He's trying to reach, but with all that He's said and done for us, the world is just too lustrous and tempting to let go of. All that is left for Him to do is remove the unworthy from among His people, and that is when God gives up on us. After trying day after day, year after year, without a hint of a change of mind, He gives up on these peculiar "Christians".

Now think with me—this kind of guest is so blatantly disrespectful to think he can come and enjoy all the richness of God's promises and still not make even the slightest sacrifice in order to fit in! No wonder they only see small blessings here and there in their lives; but the biggest and most rewarding blessings of all can only be achieved by those who truly commit to fitting into God's Kingdom. Those are the ones who make sure they look and feel appropriate in the King's presence.

Notes

_____

_____

_____

_____

_____

_____

_____

_____

_____

Bad Boy, Bad Heart

*B*ack when Abraham had received a promise from God that he would have a son and be a father of a great nation, Sarah his wife followed him around in the hope that this promise would come true some day in the near future. But as time was passing and her body was only getting older and not really showing any signs of pregnancy, Sarah started to find ways to get that promise of God fulfilled in one way or another.

She concluded that the "only way" that this promise of God could be fulfilled was to have one of her most faithful maidservants, Hagar, get pregnant on her behalf. It all made sense for her and she probably wondered why she didn't think about this earlier. She then enticed Abraham to sleep with her maidservant for that reason which was exactly what Abraham did.

It didn't take Sarah too long to realise she had made a huge mistake. Her once very nice and humble maidservant was now boasting about the whole thing and consequently despising her as the "other" unfruitful wife of Abraham. After much humiliation and disappointment, Sarah decided to be harsh with the one she had chosen to be the mother of "her son", which consequently led Hagar to flee in anger.

Eventually, Hagar returned and after giving birth to a baby boy, Ishmael, she gave him to Abraham. But you can imagine the atmosphere between those women after that. Ishmael probably grew up with many reasons from his mother to avoid Sarah, which consequently threw all her plans out the window.

Just like Sarah, many of us today know the promises of God concerning our lives, and yet can't help but follow our emotions because we can't wait for God's time. Our faith is guided by a hope from the heart, which tells us there must be a way to get this promise without needing to trust God to provide it for us. We start using our heart instead of an intelligent faith, a faith which tells us that God is in control and will eventually fulfil His promise, for He's not a man that He should speak and not accomplish it. He's God!

Sarah did not only create a problem she didn't have, but even worse, led her husband to be unfaithful to her for the first time. Abraham had been one of the few men on earth at that time who did not marry more than one wife, which was one of the reasons he was so special to God. If he could be faithful to a barren wife, he would most probably be faithful to Him.

If Sarah had only thought about what she was doing... how could God fulfil a promise making everybody's life such a mess? Why would God want Abraham to sin in order to fulfil His promise? Why would God make a great nation out of Abraham through a maidservant? It just didn't make sense. When we don't use our intelligent faith, we don't make sense at all.

Our heart wants it no matter what and we will do anything in order to get it, saying, "Forget God and His promises—time is too precious to wait and trust." And as if we had been doing the right thing from the start, we start blaming God for not doing things properly. Sarah blamed Abraham for Hagar's attitudes toward her. And in her mind, the problem was not hers but everyone's.

There you go, the story of a woman who had to learn the hard way about the difference between the faith of the heart and the faith of the spirit.

Notes

_____

_____

_____

_____

_____

Evil Heart

$\mathcal{I}$t plays us like a game. It is hard to admit it, but true. This part of us that has so much love to give, also gives us so much trouble and despair. The heart is the worst part of the human being. It doesn't care about consequences, all it cares about is its own desire. The heart has been the struggle of many men and women of God.

While intelligence concludes that it's best to stay away from the desires of our heart, our heart pushes further and further to reach its desire, making us confused and anxious at the same time. We can't sleep properly at night, thinking how we will get our heart's desire without hurting so many people at the same time.

A woman can clearly see that it's wrong to give into what her heart asks so eagerly for, and still, she can't say no because it beats stronger every time she thinks about it. Her mind searches for ways to go around it, but still, she decides there's no other way but to give in and call it a day.

Marriages and relationships end this way, and if that isn't enough, our own relationship with God ends this way, the way of the heart. It is evil beyond our understanding. All it wants is all that goes against common sense—against God. People try to give excuses by saying that they were weak or people didn't understand them, or that they just fell in love with someone else—but these are only excuses that their intelligence made up so that they could get their heart's desire without the burden of guilt on their conscience.

You and I need to acknowledge this fact: our heart is evil. It doesn't mean that we are evil; it only means that we are human and that we have to live by faith. Faith goes against emotions from the heart. It makes us feel numb to our own hearts. Whilst our heart asks for what is wrong on a daily basis, our faith tells it to shut up on a daily basis as well.

Only those who live by faith will still be in the faith when their last day arrives. Those who live by their own heart will not be around for too long because their heart, which is extremely evil, I must stress, will take them to places they will regret for the rest of their lives—places where the presence of God will no longer be found.

These are not just wise sayings or words from some book. These words come from tragic experiences I've witnessed of victims who one day were doing all they could to live a Christian life. Their own hearts deceived them dreadfully and today they are no longer in the faith. Although they may try to come back to what one-day made them the happiest people in the world, they just don't have the strength to—their heart condemns them constantly like an evil judge.

As the One who knows even the number of hairs on our head says: *"The heart is deceitful above all things, and desperately wicked; who can know it? I, the Lord, search the heart, I test the mind, even to give every man according to his ways, according to the fruit of his doings."* (Jer. 17: 9,10)

The human heart destroys more lives than the devil himself.

Notes

_____

_____

_____

_____

_____

_____

_____

_____

_____

_____

Secure and Vulnerable

$\mathcal{T}$ry to walk in the dark, making your way through a room, and see if you don't hit a couple of things on your way. Try to choose something without being able to actually see it. Try it with your eyes closed the whole time. You know it doesn't work, right? You'll stumble and hurt yourself, get extra bruises, choose the wrong thing, and even fall because you lose your balance. This is what happens when you insist on living with secrets.

Secrets bind you up. The longer they exist, the worse they get. And if that is not enough, they hold tightly on to your conscience and no matter how many times you pray and ask God to forgive you, they never leave—and do you know why? Because they are hidden in the dark, where God doesn't work.

As long as you keep holding onto things that nobody sees or hears, you reside in the dark and their influence magnifies tremendously by the minute. You're alone with all those secrets safe inside of you and yet, you are extremely vulnerable to them. And though you may think God will clear them out from your conscience, He doesn't. Not because He doesn't want to, but because He can't—they're stuck deep inside you and only you can let them go.

Removing these secrets from within requires a lot of courage, which is why many people choose to keep them safe in the dark, where no one can judge or criticise them. They lack the courage to get out of the dark and come clean, and they expect God to do that for them in secret—sorry, but God doesn't work that way.

"For everyone practicing evil hates the light and does not come to the light, lest his deeds should be exposed. But he who does the truth comes to the light, that his deeds may be clearly seen, that they have been done in God." (Jo. 3:20-21)

Even when your deeds were nothing to be proud of, as a person of God, you are clear. You shouldn't have anything to hide, even mistakes and weaknesses. Who is perfect among us? Who doesn't have a past she's ashamed of? Who hasn't ever done something she's embarrassed of? But when you come clean, that horrible mistake dies right there, and your exposure is painful but quick. On the other hand when you avoid that pain, thinking that you'll never have to deal with it again, it bothers you day in, and day out. Every time you pray, it's there accusing you, and since the Word of God always comes true, those secrets will come out when you least expect.

"For nothing is secret that will not be revealed, nor anything hidden that will not be known and come to light." (Lk. 8:17)

When it all comes out and your secret is discovered, it's never over quickly. Why go through all that? Why keep holding onto things that will eventually show up later on in life? Your secrets are not secure, but instead, they are building a great snare for you to fall hard on the day they are revealed. Don't give them the pleasure of seeing you fall. Come clean not only before God, but most of all before the people involved.

Notes

_____

_____

_____

_____

_____

_____

_____

_____

_____

High Heels

*Y*ou can't resist that stunning pair of shoes, though you know you will most probably wear them only a couple of times a year, but still, you go in the store to try them on—it's not like you're buying them! Then you look at yourself with those shoes in the mirror and you simply look great. You'd be crazy not to take them. Besides, if you don't take them now, you'll probably never see them again and you'll only regret it. Never mind they hurt so much; it feels like they were only made to decorate the store. But you take them anyway—completely uncomfortable and extremely overpriced.

Women will go to such lengths to look beautiful. It's in our nature to sacrifice in order to achieve beauty; think of all the diets you've starved yourself into, appointments at the salon that tore a diary page off your week, and all the beauty routines we go through everyday. It's a whole other job for us just so we can look beautiful.

I am completely in favour of women looking after themselves. I think looking her best is a woman's duty and privilege. However, if we are able to sacrifice so much for our body and appearance, how much more should we sacrifice for our inner self? When you are all right inside, everything on the outside shines and is more likely to bring you joy and satisfaction. But unfortunately, the opposite is also true. There are women who have so much beauty to show, but because of a sad countenance, vain conversation, and a troubled heart, they lose all the beauty they invested so much in.

These are the kind of women that have nothing to add to anyone's life. Their whole existence revolves around themselves and so their world is small and their talk inadequate. The only benefit they can possibly bring to anyone is their make-up, hair, and clothes, but even so, it's a temporary thing. Once they grow older, that's about it. Sure they can help a charity here and there, and even do some voluntary work, but let's face it, anyone, even drug dealers and thieves can do charity work!

If only the sacrifices women make towards their beauty went towards their spiritual life... Women would become jewels in this world, so precious and so unique! When a woman has a character that is truthful, faithful, submissive, discreet, respectable, loving, and hard working—she's already beautiful and all the make-up and high heels she likes to wear just complements her beauty. On the other hand, when a woman has no character, she may have all the beauty a woman can have, she will still be just an ordinary woman, good for a short marriage, disposable in friendships, and a great subject for gossip.

"Charm is deceitful and beauty is passing, but a woman who fears the LORD, she shall be praised." (Pr. 31:30)

If you can sacrifice your darling feet and a limited budget just so you can look great in those high heels, why not sacrifice your life to being godly and look great in everything else? Meditate on the Book that gives you a deep understanding of life, quoted here. Talk to the Guide of all guides daily—how privileged are we to go directly to the source! And practise what you know is right, keeping your heart clean and free from any evil feeling. This is how a woman of God gets a makeover every single day.

Notes

_____

_____

_____

_____

_____

_____

Size 0

iet today, diet tomorrow, the struggle is ever present for women these days. So why is it so hard to have the perfect body? This question keeps bouncing back and forth in women's minds all over the world. If we could say that there's one thing all women have in common, this would be it! Women who don't have a weight problem, still worry, and often struggle with it.

The problem with such worry is that it often shifts our attention from what's really important about ourselves. Our outer appearance often reflects what is underneath—what's in the heart. It would be useless then to keep taking care of what's on the outside if the heart is not doing that great, wouldn't it?

The Bible compares the heart to a spring of water. It can be fresh or bitter—we're the ones who choose. The apostle James said in James 3:11, *"Does a spring send forth fresh water and bitter from the same opening?"* We know that this is not possible but many of us are trying to make such a thing happen. If you catch yourself saying bitter words, thinking evil about others, and so forth, what does that say about you? Are you a spring of fresh or bitter water?

Women who completely ignore their spiritual state and focus only on their bodies which will ultimately grow old and die, are women who are running after the wind. The spirit is the one part that will live on for all eternity. It should not be taken for granted and left off as the last part to be attended to. Yet many do that. They spend hundreds each month on their hair, make-up, clothes, and treatments to enhance their figure, but when it comes to investing some of what they earn in the salvation of others, they're broke.

If they only took care of what's inside so that the outside would eventually benefit from it, they'd be the women they've always dreamed. Beautiful women we see on TV are women who have spent half a day in the beauty salon so they would look perfect for you on TV—that's all. Anyone can look beautiful with all the available treatments and make-up, but feeling good inside is what can really BE beautiful—beautiful for their family, beautiful for their customers, beautiful for those who are lost, and ultimately beautiful for God.

There is no problem in taking care of oneself. In fact, we should make sure we do that everyday. However, never let that be a priority for you. Remember that when the inside is not well, the outside will not be well either. Therefore, care for your heart. Get rid of all kinds of grudges and bad feelings you've been feeding inside your heart. Remove those little evil thoughts and feelings about others— if they harmed you or not, let go of it because after all, grudges and anger can only harm one person—the one tendering them!

Be a spiritual size 0 from now on. Let your heart be clean and ready to grow and mature into a woman of God and you'll like what you see in the mirror.

Notes

_____

_____

_____

_____

_____

_____

_____

_____

_____

_____

Closed For Life

$\mathcal{H}$ave you ever wondered how small businesses survive when they're always closed for this, closed for that? Small restaurants that are closed for lunch, small shops that are closed for a break, and so forth... some of them open late, close early, which makes them not so reliable. Well, if you have never wondered about this, you're not missing anything; it doesn't affect you, or does it?

Well, if you are applying the same principle to your life, then you are heading for a breakdown, or should I say, going bankrupt... bankrupt of love, joy, peace, and so on. People apply this principle of "closing up" in many areas of their life, which ends up costing them a high price.

If you're closed up, you're a very difficult person to live and work with. It's okay to be serious and not talkative all the time, but when you're too serious and you never take the time to talk even a little, then it's a problem, which makes you a difficult puzzle to solve.

Husbands often have a hard time with closed up wives. They never know what they're thinking and what they want. All they know is that their wives are not happy and if only they could figure out what would change that picture, they'd go for it.

Maybe you've been through a bad experience in life and then closed yourself up so that you'd never go through that again. But is that really the right approach to avoid bad experiences? Have you ever thought you might be missing out on friendships and better relationships? Protecting yourself from people around you won't stop you from getting yourself into trouble. It will only stop you from getting along with them and even making a difference in their lives.

A closed up woman can be described as a question mark. You never know how she is doing, how she feels, what she's thinking, what she wants, etc. She's mysterious, and though that can be fun for a while, it becomes annoying after some time.

I've known women who were so closed up in their problems that by the time somebody found out and tried to help them, it was too late. There have been other cases of women holding on to grudges their entire life because they simply couldn't take the time to get it off their chest with the person who hurt them (mind you that most of the time people are not even aware they've hurt you).

A woman of God knows that the more she closes up, the harder it is for her to find the right path to take, the right words to say, and the right behaviour to have. She's wise and therefore open, which is what makes her stand out from others. She's not afraid of what people think of her, she doesn't hide who she is, and will often make mistakes in front of you because after all, she's an open book.

You've got to love an open book person. She'll never hold anything against you because if she doesn't like something you said or did, she tells you. You can never find skeletons in her closet.

Notes

The "How To" of Faith

"Use your faith!"

"What do you mean, use my faith? I've been a Christian all my life and I've had faith in God for ages, how can that be the missing key in dealing with my problems?"

People from all over the world are constantly being reminded of how they should use their faith by their spiritual leaders in order to see God's power in their lives, but unfortunately many of them have had difficulties understanding how to use their faith and so things get complicated.

Faith is common to everyone. Not everyone has the same things, feels the same way, or looks the same way, but everyone has faith. We were already born with faith and that is one of the most beautiful gifts God has given to us. It's the tool He knew we would need so that even those who are stubborn to think they don't need God in their lives, can through their faith, come to know Him one day. So it's common to everyone, and yet not used by everyone.

People are often more inclined to use their emotions, which is the other thing that is common to all of us, and yet is not that effective to finding success. Our emotions are always up and down, depending solely on the circumstances around us, and often leading us to make the wrong decisions at the wrong time, and in the wrong place. Faith, on the other hand, is constant. It does not matter what is going on around us; our faith is unbeatable.

Few people know about this and that is why many have yet to see God's power in their lives. Their faith rests while their emotions are always running the show. Therefore as soon as her husband yells at her, she FEELS down. And because she's FEELING down, her day or even week ahead falls in to the same state—depressing and unbearable. Then to make matters worse, her children start having problems at school and there you go—her world is upside down once again.

Now, if the tool used in this situation were the one that actually works, that is, if she would have used her faith instead of her emotions as soon as her husband yelled those harsh words, she would have gone to another room and vented it all on God (the One who can actually help) and she would have His guidance to know how to deal with that. After those moments with God, she would be up and in faith, ready for the next challenge ahead, which would be her children. Her world would not be upside down, but the opposite, she would be taking control of her life through faith. Her whole day or week would not be ruined, and consequently her family would benefit from it.

That is why the Word of God says that the wise woman builds her home. Read Proverbs 14.1 and it goes on saying that the foolish one tears it down with her own hands—now that's deep! How many wives are tearing their family apart because of an emotion that is so strong and so silly at the same time? After everything is gone, that's when she wonders where she went wrong, or how she could have dealt with that situation in a different way. Well, now do you know?

Notes

_____

_____

_____

_____

_____

_____

_____

The Wrong Kind of Sign

She has been coming to the church for a while now and changes have been apparent in her life. Her goals, her friends, and her activities have all changed, too. Apparently, she's doing great, but there's something impeding her from conquering more spiritually and she can't pinpoint it. She goes out to evangelise, never misses a Wednesday and Sunday morning service, but still, she feels like no matter how much she does for God, she's never called by Him.

This is the state that many young women in the church are in when they start doing the Work of God. They've seen many changes in their lives that clearly made them assume they've changed and are now ready to do more for God, but changes don't necessarily mean that you're ready.

Before my encounter with the Lord Jesus, I also wanted to do the Work of God. I'd always seen myself married to a man of God and saving souls; nevertheless, my sole purpose was to have a life like my parents had. I wanted to be happily married to a man of God, and though I'd always said I wanted to save souls, the truth was that what I really wanted was to be married to a man of God; in other words, I wanted to do the Work of God so that I could be married to a man of God.

I loved the souls, but not enough to really sacrifice for them. My heart and thoughts were into getting myself a happy life. No wonder I daydreamed all the time. I also thought I knew God already, since I knew the Bible, lived a life that could clearly show I was a Christian, and basically didn't have any major problems otherwise. But in truth, I didn't know God and I had no clue what the Work of God was, until I was born of God.

My eyes opened and I began having a completely different understanding of what God, His Work, and life itself was all about. I became someone else entirely different. My heart changed from a heart focused on things for myself to a heart focused on others. I no longer wanted to do the Work of God for myself and for the sake of my future. God must have noticed me because it didn't take too long after that for me to be raised as an assistant and start doing the Work of God full time.

Some women want to have the Holy Spirit so they can work as assistants in the church. Others want to marry a pastor so they can be pastors' wives. But why? Why do you want what you're looking for? If there's any selfishness in what you want, then you're giving God the wrong sign, and right there is the answer to why you haven't received what you're looking for.

The Holy Spirit can only come upon those who will be useful in His Hands for the Kingdom of God, as witnesses of God here on earth. He doesn't come upon people who merely want to say they have the Holy Spirit or who can't wait to wear a uniform. The same thing applies to the Work of God. If your desire to do the Work of God is not entirely to save souls for the rest of your life, no matter where or how, whether you're married or not, then you can forget it. You may even marry a pastor, but you will not be doing the Work of God—you'll merely be employed. And that is where lies the difference between pastors' wives and pastors' wives, assistants and assistants.

Notes

_____

_____

_____

_____

_____

_____

_____

What is a Woman of God?

"Favour is deceitful, and beauty is vain: but a woman that feareth the Lord, she shall be praised." (Pv 31:30)

Once a young lady who was a faithful member of our church asked me to define 'woman of God' for her. I said, "A woman of God is a woman who knows God Himself and lives according to His will, which many times requires a lot of sacrifice". After hearing this simple answer, she nodded and gave me a look as if saying, "Thanks for nothing".

There are many women in the Church, even more than men, and many times I have wondered why they are not used by God as much as men are. And the only explanation I could find till now is that we women ar e very emotional beings, much more than men. One proof of this is our passion for romance, romantic movies, romantic songs, romantic attitudes, romantic stories, and so on. We cry at almost anything that touches our soul, even upon hearing a beautiful testimony of someone whose life changed by the power of God. We see everything through our emotional eyes making us almost melt within. Only God knows how many problems we have had, be it in our marriage or relationships, for being so emotional.

With all these emotions stirring 24 hours a day within us, we can hardly use our faith. And this explains why there are so many women in the church today who do not make any difference in the kingdom of God. They often call themselves women of God but when it comes to comparing them with men of God, there's a big contrast.

The reason lies within the answer I gave that church member that, "a woman of God is a woman who knows God Himself..." Many do not know Him yet. They base their conversion and even their "new birth" on emotions they felt during a prayer. The same emotions that lead them to cry over sad movies come upon them while the keyboard player is playing a beautiful instrumental background music during the prayer. And since that day, they've convinced themselves that they are born of God. How can they be women of God if they haven't even known God?

If you want to be a true woman of God, you must first know God—full stop. Even if you try changing your ways to live a more holy life, it will not make you a woman of God; you have to know HIM. For this you must set aside all your emotions and feelings and seek Him in faith—you will then be born a new creature and become a true woman of God. From then onwards, your life will make a great impact in the kingdom of God and the lives of everyone around you.

Notes

_____

_____

_____

_____

_____

_____

_____

_____

_____

_____

_____

_____

_____

_____

True Love

*H*e took her into his arms and kissed her as if there was no tomorrow and while in his arms, she trembled and wished that moment would never end—isn't that most women's dream? Sure many people say this is only possible in romantic movies and novels, but deep down, everyone wishes to experience it at least once in their lifetime. Some search for it in every relationship they find themselves in; and no sooner are they stricken by it and than it's gone.

I saw true love for the first time in my own parents' marriage. They lived as if they were always on honeymoon. One couldn't stay away from the other, especially my father, though a strong man, he seemed incomplete every time he was without his other half. After 36 years of marriage, they're still very much in love and now it's even harder to stay apart. I saw it while still very young and I desired it for myself with all my heart.

I think it's safe to say that true love is not found on every corner or in every relationship, not because people don't want it, but mostly because people don't know what it's about. People think love is about taking, receiving, acquiring, fulfilling, and benefiting themselves, while true love is entirely the opposite.

True love is giving and not expecting anything in return. It is patient and never seeking for its own good. Young girls do whatever it takes to be able to say, "I have a boyfriend". Older women go even further by committing themselves to a relationship that has no future, just so they can have a man to come home to at night. Single ladies get pregnant just to have a child of their own. This is the love people deceive themselves into: the love that wants, asks, demands, acquires, receives, and gets complicated more often than not. They're not thinking of anyone else but themselves.

When God gave His Son, He didn't do it to gain control over people in the world, but solely for people's own good, for their own salvation. This is true love, one that gives even when it's not certain of being reciprocated. It's unconditional, no matter how terrible things become. It's real, and no, it never ends.

Here's a simple way to put it, *"But I say to you, love your enemies, bless those who curse you, do good to those who hate you, and pray for those who spitefully use you and persecute you..."* (Mt 5:44). Only true love can actually put into practice such a beautiful attitude in a world where people can hate for the silliest reasons.

This is why only those who understand true love can know God. People come to God for so many reasons and they think they love Him, but deep down, they have an agenda to be fulfilled and God "must" do what He promised in their lives.

Why is it so hard to understand true love? Why isn't it more popular and attainable? Because it's not easy, and few people are willing to go through self-denial and sacrifice for others, though they'll gladly do it for their own self. They serve themselves, and so they can't, and never will find true love.

My first experience with true love was the day I met my Lord, and from then on, true love has always been with me. I have no words to describe it because only when you find it can you really understand it—and even more, give it!

Notes

_____

_____

_____

_____

_____

_____

_____

_____

A Special Glow

The minute she enters a room, it immediately brightens up and her glow is visible to all present there. People can't explain what it is that makes them fixated by the way she talks and smiles. It is inevitable that when her eyes meet your eyes, it draws a smile to her face—not necessarily because she knows you but because it is the way she is, it is her glow.

You feel so special when she talks to you and the way she makes you feel. It is as if you were so important and yet you know you are just like everyone else. And when she is sad, it is almost impossible to tell, unless you are very close to her and that is because she loves to be a happy person.

She is also very secure about herself and everything she does. No wonder many other women try to become like her. It is not her beauty or popularity that draws them, but this glow that just seems to always be there, shining out for everyone to see.

Have you ever met someone like this? Isn't it a privilege to know her? You wish you were closer to her, you wish you knew her better, you wish she would be your mentor, you wish you were her. So what is so special about her? What is this glow that isn't something you find in everyone and is so rarely obtained?

It is the Holy Spirit. A person who is filled by the Spirit of God has this natural glow inside of them. It is fruitful and everybody enjoys its fruit. The fruit of the Holy Spirit *"...is love, joy, peace, longsuffering, kindness, goodness, faithfulness, gentleness, self-control."* (Gal 5:22,23)

That is the glow the woman of God has. Not every woman has it, not every woman sees the need to have it, not every woman seeks for it, and that is why it is so rare to find and so special when found.

I have known women with this glow and I can truly say they stand out from all other women I know.

Her love towards God and everything He has created makes it easy to spot because she lives to show this love. Her joy is natural and never forced. Her peace even in troublesome times brings comfort to others. Her patience with those who are weaker in the faith describes her spiritual motherhood. Her kindness towards everyone regardless of his or her colour or nationality is much appreciated. Her goodness in serving everyone and anyone that comes her way clearly shows her servitude. Her faithfulness towards the responsibilities she gains throughout her life shows her excellent spirit. Her gentleness in speaking and dealing with others draws people closer to her. And last but not least, her self-control whenever things get out of hand describes her spiritual maturity.

Many women say they have the Holy Spirit but how can that be if they are always so sad, angry, disturbed, anxious, moody, cruel, unfaithful, and rude? It is very clear to me that those who have the Holy Spirit bear His fruit. How can it be otherwise?

There are women that can actually put you down instead of lift you up. There are women who make you feel ashamed to know they are part of the church. They are never happy because someone else is; they are never good towards anyone that is not of their family. Any responsibility given to them will surely get stuck, as they are just too self-centred to get anything done that is not meant for them.

Want to have that special glow? Seek the Holy Spirit and only be sure He is present in your life when you can see His fruit clearly visible in you.

Notes

_____

_____

_____

_____

_____

True Colours

There are pop songs and poems about it, but still, how hard it is to see a person's true colours nowadays. People grow up and learn of ways to hide their real self from others either out of self-protection or the need to gain respect.

We open magazines and newspapers and we see people smiling at the cameras as if they were the happiest people on earth but that couldn't be farther from the truth. All too often, these same people are the ones who can't sleep at night or ever have a permanent relationship. They get drunk from time to time to forget their problems, or get a jail sentence for drug abuse or stealing, or even end up committing suicide later on in life.

One of the things God searches for the most in us human beings is the sincerity of our hearts. We can only know God when we open ourselves up to Him. It is not because God does not know us, for He knows even how many hairs we have on our head. The truth is that when we open up, we automatically empty ourselves of all that has kept us in a masquerade—we open our hearts.

Many people have a hard time understanding what it means to open their hearts to God. They often hear this when they go to church and some may think it is just a cliché that pastors use. But that isn't so. As mentioned before, you can only know God when you open yourself up.

As long as a woman holds onto her mask—in other words, pride—God cannot help her. She can pray, fast, and make special purposes, and still God will not be reached.

God knows each one of us inside out, more even than we know ourselves, so why hide who we really are? Why put on a mask and pretend we can still make it without Him? Why go deeper into the pit? Haven't we seen enough sorrow? The truth is that not being sincere with God is simply being a fool before Him!

There are those who like to live their lives in a pretence of happiness. No matter what is going on in their marriages, in their financial lives, in their spirit, or even in their darkest moments. All that matters to them is to get others to think they are happy and live a perfect life—but who does? Even Christian, born of God, Spirit-filled women go through problems from time to time so that they can exercise their faith.

"A man's pride will bring him low, but the humble in spirit will retain honour." (Pv 29:23)

Our true colours are visible to God and sometimes even to those who belong to Him, and only a fool would try to hide it. Be yourself and let God work in you. By all means, do use make up but don't make it a mask for your life!

Notes

_____

_____

_____

_____

_____

_____

_____

_____

_____

_____

_____

_____

Relationships That Work

Can you honestly say that you're close to someone you hardly ever speak to? You might like that person and even feel a special care for her, but you don't know her as well as you know someone you're always with. This is because a relationship requires communication. No one endures a relationship based only on what one person means to the other.

A couple needs their time alone to talk, so do children, and so do best friends. Anyone who means anything to us requires some time alone to talk. The conversation does not necessarily have to be about the relationship, but it's still extremely important to keep that relationship going.

It's no different with God. Many Christians boast about their belief in God and yet don't have a relationship with Him. They are busy Christians. Their 24 hours are filled with everything else but God, though they come to church a few hours a week, they think that it's enough to keep their Christian title up.

Can you have a relationship with your husband if you only speak with each other twice a week? I don't think so. If that is happening, most probably those rare times are mainly arguments! If your relationship with God is based on a belief and nothing else, it only means that this relationship won't stand a chance. And when things don't go according to plan in your life, this relationship won't go according to plan either.

Just like in any relationship, you need to communicate with God in order to have a relationship with Him. He is not worried whether you call yourself a Christian or not, because that alone doesn't make you a Christian. You are only a true Christian when you know God personally and your relationship with Him is real.

A woman of prayer is of great value to God because He knows that she takes time just to speak to Him, though she's constantly busy with so many things in her life. If you are a parent, you know that it's a bad sign if your child stops interacting with you. It's the same thing with God. You may even hold an important title in the church, but if you don't talk to God as often as you talk to everyone else in your life, your relationship with Him is poor and needy.

To illustrate this, the Lord Jesus said in Matthew 7:22 and 23, *"Many will say to Me in that day, 'Lord, Lord, have we not prophesied in Your name, cast out demons in Your name, and done many wonders in Your name? And then I will declare to them, 'I never knew you; depart from Me, you who practice lawlessness!'"*

Some people read this verse and don't realise how strong it is. Our Lord is actually saying that many Christians will go to hell! And if those who served Him are mentioned here, imagine those who didn't serve Him at all?

Let us be wise and stop faking a relationship, which ought to mean so much more than just a religion in our lives. Set aside time everyday, preferably when you know that no one else will interrupt, to talk to God. You will soon notice how strong and spiritually fulfilled you'll be, being close to the One that can actually fulfil all your needs.

Notes

_____

_____

_____

_____

_____

_____

_____

_____

_____

The Evil Queen

Sometimes people think it's an overstatement to say that women have the power to either raise a man up or put him down. The Word of God speaks of various examples of women of both kinds, but there's one in particular that is not so often mentioned and did horrible things in the Kingdom of Israel in her day. This woman, called Athalia, was royalty (read 2 Chronicles 22). She was the granddaughter of one of Israel's failed kings and eventually married a king in Israel and had a son named Azaiah, who also became a king after his father's death.

Just like his father and mother, Azaiah did not fear God and did evil in his days, and as a result of that, he died young. Athalia, on the other hand, wasn't ready to be a thing of the past. All that luxury she had enjoyed while in the "White House" was just too good to let go of, so she decided to kill all the royal heirs and take over the kingdom with her own hands. Yes, that's right—kill innocent children for the sake of more power! It was like this woman went mad. She wasn't thinking about the consequences that were probably going to make her look bad in the eyes of the people of Israel, let alone in God's eyes.

I am sure that Athalia had never imagined herself one day going as far as being a murderer in order to keep her kingdom. This is what happens to women who don't know who they really are. They are capable of anything and that is dangerous. It's not that her background was rough or anything, after all, she had been born into a royal family. She had everything. She had the best education and the best of everything in the kingdom, but that wasn't enough to make her a good person.

The fact is that a woman who does not know who she is, does not know what she is capable of. You never know how she will react to different situations in her life and that can many times be scary. It is almost as if you're walking on eggshells when you're next to her. Her feelings about you are never truly known. One day she likes you so much; the other day she hates you so much. Who is this woman? Not even she knows who she is, so don't be surprised.

You can only expect good from a woman who is sure of herself, and that quality can only be found in a woman of God. There may be women in the world who say they know themselves pretty well, but in fact, they don't, because if they did, they would know that the best thing they could ever do in their lives was to know God. They keep trying to make it without Him and they're never fulfilled.

The woman of God knows who she is. She is certain of what is ahead of her. She's not psychic, but her faith keeps her calm for the days to come. Nothing and no one can remove this assurance from within her because this certainty comes from above. If you want to have this certainty within yourself, just go to the source of it all—your Creator, who in turn will make you the person He meant you to be right from the beginning!

Notes

_____

_____

_____

_____

_____

_____

_____

_____

_____

_____

The Day I Was Born

It was a lovely Sunday morning. I was sitting in the front row of the church and thought I had it all. I had been in church throughout my childhood. I knew all the stories of the Bible and had all the knowledge of what was wrong and right. There I was, a teenager who didn't do drugs, didn't get involved with the wrong crowd, didn't go to parties or discos, didn't drink, didn't have a boyfriend, and didn't even lie.

The bishop, who by the way was my father, spoke about the parable of the wheat and all of a sudden my heart was pumping stronger than usual. I didn't know why I was getting the impression that I was the weed and not the wheat. I couldn't understand it; after all, I was basically a "saint"! What could possibly make me feel like I didn't belong among the wheat, that is, the children of God?

And that was when the bishop called those who realised their spiritual state before God and wanted to have a true encounter with God, to come forward. All kinds of thoughts came in my mind at that moment. If I went forward, my family and friends would see me go and find out that I had been a deceiver. I was ashamed and even thought of staying behind and making my prayer from my seat. However something was telling me to break my pride in order to know God personally. I had to give up something and that was my image before others.

So I went forward. I felt the eyes of the whole church looking straight at me, but I was determined to place that whole "saint" image behind me and just be who I really was before God. That was the last minute of my old life. I was 15 when I had a true encounter with the Lord Jesus Christ.

I wasn't full of sins, but I was a sinner. I wasn't in the wrong, but I was wrong. All my life I had heard about Someone whom I had never met until that day. It was the happiest day of my life. I couldn't hold back my tears and when the prayer had finished, I wanted to hug everyone around me and go up on a hill and tell the whole world about the Lord Jesus. I just couldn't stop smiling as if I had gone back to being a child.

After that day, I realised how empty I used to be. How insecure and afraid I was. I had so many evil thoughts and my thoughts of the future were so futile and doubtful. I couldn't understand what the deal was about church, Holy Spirit, and even God. I knew that was the way to go, but I just didn't really know why.

I was a new Cristiane. Everything made sense; it became clear and simple after that. I wasn't afraid to speak about the Lord Jesus anymore because now I really knew Him! I just became a completely new me—the woman I am today.

When I look back, before I was born, it even seems like I used to be someone else, to live someone else's vain life. It's almost impossible to describe the change that happened deep inside. Only when you're truly born of God can you understand.

People sometimes have a hard time understanding why they're still not born of God. There are no secrets. Just simply give up your pride and realise the need so God can do the rest.

Notes

_____

_____

_____

_____

_____

_____

_____

_____

The Unforgettable

*N*ot everybody is out there to make a difference. There are those whom you'll know for being "okay" and those whom you'll never forget. These people are the unforgettable ones, those whose lives meant something to you. They weren't just anybody—they made a difference.

It is much simpler to live one's life to the fullest and let others struggle through theirs by themselves, that is, everyone taking care of their own business. However a woman who wants to make a difference in the world does not feel right focusing exclusively on her life. She knows that in order to make a difference she will have to go out of her way and touch other lives as well.

This is why there aren't many names that will spring to mind when we think of people who made a difference in our lives. They were unique, they were extraordinary, they did something nobody had ever done, and they were different.

It is not easy to be unique and do things that people in general wouldn't normally dare to. They have to face all kinds of obstacles such as misunderstanding, criticism, wrongful accusations, and so much more. That is because whenever you step out of the ordinary you automatically stand out, and that obviously puts you in the spotlight. All of a sudden, everybody's eyes are upon you trying to understand you, trying to find the reason why you're drawing so much attention to yourself.

People won't hold their tongues from criticising and judging you when they see how well you're doing and how they secretly wished they were in your shoes. The minute you come out of your comfort zone and start making a difference, that's the minute you'll start being misunderstood. Only those who are willing to go the extra mile and sacrifice their comfort and trouble-free zone can actually make a difference and be unforgettable.

There were many South Africans during the time of apartheid that felt revolted and angry at that system of discrimination, but only a few who actually did something about it. At the time, they were probably misunderstood and criticised even by their loved ones, but today, their names stand out in history. People from all over the world know Nelson Mandela, who was effortlessly voted into office for president after the apartheid era. Why? Because he stood out and went the extra mile, not caring about what people thought or what would eventually be the consequences of his actions. He's one of the unforgettables of our times.

You don't need to be jailed or be beaten up to make a difference. If you'll only be honest with a friend to point out some of the things that are clearly wrong that will eventually harm her later on, you're making a difference in her life. She may not understand you and may even think wrongly of you, but nothing better than time to reveal the truth and make people realise how unforgettable you really are. You were a real friend, someone who cared enough to tell the truth and not worry about your own image or ego.

Some people think it's too stressful to make a difference in someone's life and that prayers alone will do it. I, on the other hand, thank God for having had real friends who didn't just pray for me, but were courageous enough to help me see the things I couldn't see. I'll never forget them—they'll always be in my heart.

"Open rebuke is better than love carefully concealed." (Pv. 27.5)

Notes

_____

_____

_____

_____

_____

_____

Her Assets

"Did you see how she looked at me?" "I'm never going to speak to him again!" "I can seek God at home—after all, isn't He everywhere?"

Unaware of what really matters, people often throw one of their most valuable assets down the drain: their faith. Little things here and there are enough to compromise their faith, leaving them like an empty shell, beautiful but useless. So much potential, such a promising future ahead, but they just can't stand the little irritations, as if these would make such a big difference in their lives.

Why are we so foolish at times? I guess we can say we don't realise how important our faith really is. We think little things can't damage it, whilst in fact these spread fast throughout our heart leading to a spiritual cancer hard to be detected. People who are affected by such a spiritual disease cannot be healed, not because there's no healing for it, but because they don't realise they have a problem. For them, the problem lies with everybody else and they are just "poor victims".

Faith is the most valuable asset anyone can ever have. Without it, we're doomed to failure, no matter how rich we are. It is the only way for anyone to get to God and without it, you might as well live as if God didn't exist. My dear friend, cherish your faith. Don't diminish it because of something someone said or did; don't lose it because you're too self-conscious about how you stand before God. No one deserves anything from Him and if it weren't for the faith God has given us, we'd be spiritually dead.

To guard your faith is the wisest thing you can ever do for yourself. Guard it from gossip, evil eyes, misunderstandings, malicious conversations, doubts, and so many other enemies of your faith. It's useless to come to church and live a "Christian life" if this faith is nowhere to be found in your heart. Some people lost it years ago, no wonder their life shows the complete opposite of what God has promised in His Word.

Where is your faith right now? How does it stand? Don't be foolish to think that those "little" sins here and there can be overlooked—or don't you know that the little foxes are the ones that spoil the vines? Read Song of Solomon 2:15. Think about it—is it really worth the trouble getting angry or bitter because of the way she looked at you, or the way he spoke to you? One can only consider herself spiritually mature when she turns a blind eye to other peoples' faults so her faith will not be contaminated.

Someone once asked, "Why don't I see the promises of God in my life?" The most probable answer to this question is the kind of faith she has been living. There's faith and there's faith. One hundred per cent faith and a somewhat fake one that some Christians live nowadays.

Faith that is kept intact, in another words, unaffected by the various circumstances in this world, is the one that takes us to victory. Everything else is useless.

Notes

_____

_____

_____

_____

_____

_____

_____

_____

_____

_____

_____

Game Over

Nobody likes to lose. Sure, some people will say they play just for the fun of it, but they know that in reality they would appreciate it very much if they had won the game, whatever game it was. We play because we want to win; it's as simple as that. Now I wonder why some people don't follow the same "obvious" rule in their own life.

They work hard, spend precious time with their loved ones, and do everything they could possibly do to live a life that is good and acceptable just to say at the end of the day, "Well, I've done my best so I might as well be happy with the little and insignificant life I have." Come on! Why do you give so much and get so little? Don't you ever get tired of it? I would.

Someone will say, "But that's my faith; I don't have the faith to conquer", and I ask, then what kind of faith is that? Faith was given to us to conquer—not only eternal life, but also a life that can lead others to eternal life, or do you think that you'll be a good witness of God living a rubbish life?

People who hate church and Christianity often say, "Christians are weak" which is an outrageous idea to live with. And yet, in light of what we see in the life of some Christians, we can only keep our mouths shut. If it's humiliating for us, imagine what it's like for God? How ashamed does He feel whenever one of His children lives a miserable life and is fine with it?

If you're a mother, you know how embarrassing it is to see your child clothed in old and ragged clothes, whilst all the other children around him look great. You feel, as though you're the one wearing those old clothes, as a matter of fact, you're more ashamed than the child.

It's not enough to be good—you won't testify of the Lord Jesus by being good. You want to talk about Him? You want to do His Work? What have you got to show others then? Anyone can speak about God, but not everyone can show Him. Besides, if you can't even achieve material blessings, how will you achieve eternal ones?

Have you ever wondered why God created us? It wasn't to make us His little toys or to be entertained by our various struggles in life. God created us to bring Him glory: a child that would have the free will to decide to live his life for Him. He's only glorified when that is a reality. Forget about worship and praise ministries! Those can only mean something for God when they are true in the person's life. How can you praise God if you're living in hell at home? Or when you're depressed every other day? Or when you cannot afford to buy your daily bread?

To summarise it all, you've got to live to conquer so that when this life is over, you may have lived it to the fullest. Your children will want to follow in your footsteps. Your friends will see the difference in you. Your enemies will be overthrown just by looking at your life. You'll be bringing yourself a true sense of achievement. And most important of all, you'll be fulfilling the purpose of why you exist—to glorify God with your life. Game Over.

Notes

_____

_____

_____

_____

_____

_____

_____

_____

In Need of Some Eye Drops?

*A*s that beautiful young girl went up onto the altar to give her testimony, a sudden, unexpected look came from behind where she was sitting. The look made her blush and look down as she stepped closer to the pastor. That pair of eyes, staring at her from top to bottom, were almost telling her to sit down and be quiet. And where was that look coming from? Another frustrated young girl.

Have you ever tried to work on something whilst looking at someone else's work? It's impossible to get anything done whilst you're not concentrating on your own work. The results never come out right. The same thing happens in life and unfortunately, this is where many women fail. Many of them can't take their eyes off other women—the way they dress, the way they walk, what they do in life, who their husband is, how much they weigh, what colour their hair is, and so on. Women are fascinated by other women. No wonder women's magazines sell so well!

The problem is that whilst a woman is so concerned about the woman next door, she's not really looking at herself.

Those who are not looking at what others do or don't do are usually the ones going forward and envied by those who just can never move on in life.

In Mathew 6:22—7:5, the Lord Jesus speaks about this: *"The lamp of the body is the eye. If therefore your eye is good, your whole body will be full of light. But if your eye is bad, your whole body will be full of darkness. If therefore the light that is in you is darkness, how great is that darkness!...Judge not, that you be not judged. For with what judgment you judge, you will be judged;*

and with the measure you use, it will be measured back to you. And why do you look at the speck in your brother's eye, but do not consider the plank in your own eye? Or how can you say to your brother, 'Let me remove the speck from your eye'; and look, a plank is in your own eye? Hypocrite! First remove the plank from your own eye, and then you will see clearly to remove the speck from your brother's eye."

The minute we start looking at other people's lives, we can't help but judge them. We judge them because that's what happens when our eyes are focused on something other than the will of God and ourselves. This could be the reason why your blessing is kind of stuck—you work, sacrifice, do everything you are taught (almost everything considering the above), and you just can't reach it. You keep telling yourself that God knows the right time for things, and you're absolutely right—you're not ready for that blessing yet! If you can't keep your eyes off other people, especially those of the same faith, how can you even see what's right in front of you?

Pointing fingers will not solve anything and judging will do even less. One of the greatest turn offs in women is their constant craving to badmouth other women, especially if they're more successful or beautiful than they are. No man tolerates that because it's a low shot that shows how insecure and inadequate such woman is. Imagine what God thinks!

Notes

Nonsense Beauty

Try to picture a pig wallowing in mud with a diamond ring in its nose. These two don't go together, do they? But that is how the Bible describes women who don't have discretion (read Proverbs 11:22). Harsh, but very true.

According to the dictionary, discretion means, "the quality of behaving or speaking in such a way as to avoid causing offence or revealing private information". In other words, it means the ability to discern good from bad, both in words and deeds.

Some women don't realise how important discretion is for their own image. They keep trying to show so much goodness and gentleness, but when it comes to being discreet, they can't. So they easily gossip about other people, criticise others, and talk about private matters to people who have nothing to do with them.

They often joke with the wrong people, at the wrong time, with the wrong words.

Others have a hard time keeping themselves in their place. They don't realise how horrible it is for a lady to yell and speak loudly to others, to flirt with committed men, and to be rude to their loved ones in public. And let us not forget those who are indiscreet in the way they dress, as if their bodies were an amusement centre for all males.

These women are beautiful and yet because of their talk and attitudes, their beauty is just vain. It's just like when you hear about a scandal involving a very famous person. Every time you see or hear about that person, you quickly remember the scandal involving her in the past. And the image of her in your mind is quickly shattered. Due to her indiscretion, her beauty is no longer appreciated!

Discretion also means avoiding getting yourself into trouble. Think about it. Let us use the examples given already.

1. Gossip and criticism of others—also means that you most probably have few friends and the friends you have most probably do not trust you either. When one gossips about someone else with you, she certainly gossips about you to others.

2. Sharing private matters with others—also means that you cannot be trusted with any important confidential information and that your family is usually the victim of your unnecessary comments about them.

3. Uncalled-for jokes—simply makes you look like a fool and fools are not pleasant people to be around.

4. Yelling and speaking loudly to others—also means that you're throwing all your femininity down the drain and that you're very hard to deal with.

5. Flirting with committed men—do we really need to mention what kind of trouble you'll be bringing upon yourself here?

6. Being rude to your loved ones—also means that if you are rude to those who are closest to you, imagine those who are not!

7. Indiscretion in the way you dress—can also mean that you desperately need attention. Some women have been raped or sexually abused because of the way they were dressed.

Let us be common-sense beauties—after all, to be compared to a pig's snout is something no woman should ever be proud of!

Notes

_____

_____

_____

_____

_____

_____

_____

She Understands

Someone said something you didn't like and that comment or gossip keeps jumping up and down inside your heart, making it hard to forgive and forget. You are deeply disappointed with someone you highly esteemed because he has done something that hurt you profoundly. Just the other day, you heard somebody who does not even know you, talking behind your back and you felt completely misjudged—and the list of how you get hurt goes on and on. It's almost as if there is no one good out there and you begin to wonder if you should expect the worst from everybody around you.

"...There is none good but one, that is, God." (Mt. 19:17) Most people know but don't realise this concept. They think it only applies to strangers or people of bad character, but no: the Bible is very clear about the "none good", which includes you and me! No one is good, except the Father. Everyone has shortcomings and weaknesses. There is always something we haven't learned or haven't experienced yet in order to do better and so we make mistakes. It's a fact of life and those who are spirit know and understand this.

When a person is spirit, that is, born of God, she understands those around her because she looks at things differently. Naturally she feels angry and revolted at the time, but that anger and revolt does not last a day because her spirit is in control. Nevertheless, when a person is flesh, that is, born of the flesh, she doesn't understand people around her. It is very hard for her not to keep a grudge inside her heart because her emotions speak louder than her spirit.

This is the difference between Christians and Christians. Christians who are born of the spirit behave like the Spirit, think like

God, and act like Him. Christians who are born of the flesh behave the way any other person in this world would behave, think the way they have always thought, and act the way they think is best. Many of them are full of grudges, envy, jealousy, and pride which are some of the most common things in this world.

These evil feelings come exactly because of their inclination to do the things of the flesh and live according to their soul's desire. They are not evil, but they do evil. They don't want to harm anyone, but they harm the ones closest to them. Some children have complete disgust for the things of God exactly because of their mothers' bad testimony at home. Some husbands feel unworthy of ever stepping foot in the church because their wives, who are very active members in the church, are always boasting of how "holy" they are and how "unholy" their husbands are. Women full of pride, think they are doing God a favour by being this way.

Those who are born of God never make others feel small, but on the contrary, they understand those who are still in darkness, and even more, those who are pretending to be of God and are not. They understand as God understands and is patient with them. One day, they'll wake up from their deep sleep and realise how lost they have been and finally seek the new birth.

Notes

_____

_____

_____

_____

_____

_____

_____

_____

_____

_____

Simply Cursed?

She ran up to the pastor on that dark night and told him how up-set she was. The woman was trembling all over as she exhorted him to be friendlier to the congregation. She explained that she didn't mean to upset or criticise him, but she was just concerned about the church and how his different way of dealing with the members was just not acceptable. This member had been active in the church for years and faithful in her tithes and offerings, which therefore led her to conclude that it was her duty to come forth and pronounce her dissatisfaction towards her new pastor.

It is not uncommon to see this happening every now and again in churches all over the world. In every church, there's always that group of people who think the church owes them for all their effort and faithfulness throughout the years. It saddens me to con-clude that because of their demands, they show that all they've done and continue to do is for mere men, whilst God, whom they really owe their lives to, gets nothing, except this petty kind of behaviour towards others.

If only they realised that pastors, pastors' wives, assistants, and everyone else who belong to the Church of the Lord Jesus Christ are merely men and women doing their best to serve Him despite all their human weaknesses. These people were taken from the darkness one day and placed in the light, not because they de-served it, but because they were chosen. If God chose them, who are we to question?

Nevertheless, this group of people insist on questioning those who were chosen by God. Just like Miriam questioning the authority of Moses when he made the mistake of marrying a woman who was not of Israelite blood. Miriam was faithful and very independent in her faith, but when she talked about Moses behind his back, God became furious with her and she immediately became leprous. Read Numbers 12.

"Why then were you not afraid to speak against My servant Moses?" (Nu. 12:8)

It's not that Moses was right in marrying that foreign woman. However, God, who had chosen him, was the One to deal with him and no one else. After all, what good can come of private criticism and useless blabber? As a matter of fact, only curses can come of that, which may be the reason why some people who work so hard struggle with some outrageous problems in their life—a disease out of the blue, a sudden problem in their marriage, and other problems they'd never imagined God would allow to happen. But He does. It's written and God made sure to say it right in the beginning of times, when He chose Abraham, *"I will bless those who bless you, And I will curse him who curses you."* (Ge. 12:3)

This is a promise made by God to all those who serve Him. However, when a servant of God goes against another servant of God, he stops serving God, which opens the way for curses to come upon his life. You can be the most faithful member or assistant in the church, but if you speak against someone else in the church, your faithfulness is worth nothing. Keep your tithes and offerings because God will reject them any way. He said, *"Therefore if you bring your gift to the altar, and there remember that your brother has something against you, leave your gift there before the altar, and go your way. First be reconciled to your brother, and then come and offer your gift."* (Mt. 5:23-24)

Don't bring unnecessary curses upon yourself. Rebuke those evil thoughts and give your concerns to God and let Him decide what needs to be changed and how.

Of course, you should and must report any bad behaviour by church workers as part of your zeal for the Work of God. The way to do this is to report to the person in authority who is in charge of the person concerned.

Notes

The Gracious Woman

*Y*ou go out on a deserved break after a long day of hard work hoping to unload the stresses of your job, only to be mistreated and humiliated by the shopkeeper, or the driver behind you, or even the church member who is angry because you sat in her seat. It is frustrating to have to put up with so much rudeness nowadays, but as the Lord Jesus said about the end of times, *"...The love of many will grow cold."* (Mt. 24:12) This is just the beginning of worse times!

Love, for many, is just a word in a song or some fantasy feeling people die for, but for those who are of God, it is true and apparent to everyone around them, not only to Christians but everyone, including strangers. Their love is not conditional to the weather or how lucky they feel that day—it is unconditional to the circumstances around them. There are millions and millions of women in this world and among these, are those who are gracious women of God. They have this love inside that urges them to serve and please others, even when they know that they will never be repaid for all they've done.

The Bible says that gracious women retain honour (Pv. 11:16); in other words, they hold on to their honour, and though they may go through tribulations and misunderstanding, their honour is never touched. Unlike many others who are not interested in being kind to others, gracious women do not bring shame on themselves, their husbands or their children. Conversely, women without graciousness are never honoured because of their badmouthing, constant criticism, rudeness, impatience, nervousness, and the usual long face.

Some may say that due to their hard work and many sacrifices, they deserve respect and honour from their children, friends, or relatives but how can anyone respect an evildoer or speaker? I have heard women talk about God and the Bible many times but the only ones that truly blessed me were the ones I saw live God and the Bible in their lives. These women are special and worthy of honour and respect. It is not what you preach, but what you live. If you consider yourself a woman of God and still allow yourself to be rude, to tell a gossip, and be inconsiderate to others, you have not yet known the God you say you belong to.

God is love, but not just love, He's the real thing—His love is unconditional and never changes. People may reject Him and say they don't believe in Him, and yet He loves them. What kind of love have you given to others lately? The one that is only present in speech and songs, or this kind of love that gives without expecting anything back, the kind that makes someone else's day and not necessarily yours?

The gracious woman is cordial, courteous, polite, well-mannered, civil, affable, sociable, congenial, kind, generous, benign, benevolent, merciful, compassionate, humane, charitable, and understanding. These are all synonyms of being gracious. Think about that. It might just be the missing piece to your husband's, parents', friends', brothers', or children's conversion.

Notes

_____

_____

_____

_____

_____

_____

_____

_____

_____

_____

Part 2

*From Single
to Married
Life*

My Youth

$\mathcal{B}$eing young and full of life can be a snare sometimes. I remember when I thought I had all the time in the world ahead of me to do whatever I wanted with my life, to be whoever I wanted to be, to have all the fun I could have, and enjoy the secret adventure I thought I would go through in the future. But all that strength and hope I thought I had wasn't always there. There were nights I felt so lonely and days I felt like going to my bedroom and staying there until dawn.

My family thought I had it all under control. My desires seemed to be the right ones, so they thought; but only God knew what went through my mind constantly. Nobody knew how hard it was for me to grow out of all the evil thoughts that took unwanted residence in my head. I did well in school and I didn't go with the wrong crowds, but in my mind, I did. I wanted to be like them, to have what they had—all the fun they talked about when they went out on Friday nights. Deep inside, I wanted that life and though I knew it was wrong, I thought I had the right to enjoy my youth just like everybody else did. The world's lights were extremely attractive to my eyes and I just wanted to be part of it.

It was only when I met God that I finally realised that all those shining lights were not as shiny as they seemed. I started to see the world with different eyes: a lost world. MTV videos weren't fun to watch anymore. The glamorous actresses weren't that glamorous anymore. I didn't depend on music to breathe anymore. It was like I was suddenly living in another world, a crazy world that once was part of who I was, but now was too cra zy for me.

My friends started thinking that I became a fanatic because the pleasures of this world weren't my pleasures anymore. Suddenly, my Walkman had no purpose! I would lie in bed and just sleep. I didn't need to listen to music until the late hours of the night to fall asleep anymore. I was still young but different from most of the young people I knew; they couldn't understand me but I could understand them. They criticised me and I prayed for them in return.

Today, many years have passed and I am not a teenager anymore, but I see teenagers everywhere, some living the life I once lived—moved by music and the latest fashion. They have the same view of life: enjoy it while you're young and full of life. Little do they know that all their enjoyment will bring future consequences they'll regret terribly. I was blessed to have met God before making a big mistake in life, but it wasn't because I was lucky—it was because I listened to His voice when He spoke to me for the first time.

God speaks—in every service, sometimes in songs, and even through other people's experiences. If you want to, you can listen; but if you don't want to, one day, it might be too late.

Notes

Young and Blessed

Going to school was not easy for my sister or me. We did not speak the native language and kids looked down on us because of where we came from. We could not wait to get home and be in each other's company and have our lovely mother take care of us.

Our mother made it all seem so easy that when we remember those days, we even miss them! Since we were young, she taught us that we were born to glorify our Lord and because of that, we would be different from everybody else. And we indeed grew up thinking that way. Whilst everybody in school hated and disrespected their parents, we loved and honoured ours.

One can expect hatred and disrespect from a teenager who does not have faith in God, but never from a Christian one. And there are still those who come to church, get involved in all kinds of activities in church, show a lot of respect to the pastors and assistants, and yet do not honour their own mother and father.

God was very clear when He said in Exodus 20:12, *"Honour your father and your mother, that your days may be long upon the land which the LORD your God is giving you."* One can conclude from this, one of the 10 commandments, that if you cannot honour those who are your own parents in flesh, how could you honour Him Who is your Parent in spirit?

Many young people today are suffering with all kinds of problems. They don't understand why they are depressed for no apparent reason, angry at the world and everybody in it. They're dying so young and full of life. Why?

Let's take the verse above and put it the other way around. "Dishonour your father and your mother, that your days may be short upon the land which the LORD your God will be giving you." Get it?

And again I say, all the prayers and all that you do for God will be in vain when you don't practise the most basic of His commandments. Many mothers have come to us for advice on how to handle their teenage daughter who is very active in the church but so inactive at home. They care so much for their children and make all kinds of sacrifices on their behalf only to receive in turn, a long face, a sharp tongue, complete disrespect, and a scornful look at the end of the day.

Mothers who pray for their families deserve all the honour and respect from their children. They wouldn't be where they are now if it weren't for their mothers who many times lost out so their children could gain. They suffered so their children would not, and cried so that the children would laugh.

The youth who truly honour their parents will always be young and blessed as far as God is concerned. It does not matter if their parents come to church or not, are good or evil, are worthy or not—they are parents and that is enough for them to be respected.

In school, girls used to make fun of us because of how much we loved our parents. These same girls today are unhappy women whose children probably also hate them. And we, well, we grew up to be very happy women indeed!

Notes

_____

_____

_____

_____

_____

_____

_____

A Girl's Story

It's the same old story. Boy meets girl, girl falls in love with boy, and he asks her to sleep with him in order to prove her love. Girl gives in so she won't lose the boy of her dreams and after a little while, he drops her for someone else and now she is no longer a girl but a mother-to-be.

And for some time, this girl does not want anything to do with boys because she is just too hurt to get into any relationship. But as soon as the moment has passed, she has fallen for someone else, and this time she tells herself that she will not lose him. Then it happens again, her roof falls in on her and she's alone one more time. "What will my friends think of me?" she says. "What will my family say this time? Something must be wrong with me!"

As long as she gives in to anyone that comes her way, there will always be something wrong, because the most intimate area of her life is at the disposal of anyone who knocks on her door!

Sex is the most intimate and personal a person can get with someone else, and it shouldn't be shared with just any man or boyfriend. It's the bond that makes a couple become one only after marriage. When you try to make this bond with someone who is not your husband, neither of you will become one, and consequently will end up separate because of the nonsense that it is: of the flesh.

Many women do not realise how important it is for sex to exist only after marriage. They think it is a desire of the flesh and just too strong to be controlled, but deep down the desire of the flesh is not actually sex itself, but the desire to have the man of her dreams at whatever cost, and sex becomes a tool for her.

You watch movies and TV nowadays and sex is everywhere. Everybody does it, everybody talks about it, everybody sings about it, but in reality few people really understand its importance and meaning. That is because God Himself created it.

He created it so that both man and woman would become one for the rest of their lives like He is One (Father, Son, and Holy Spirit). This oneness is so great that He made it possible for us to have the same oneness when we come into a real commitment called marriage.

A girl can dream of her prince but if she does not make herself a princess, how can she ever find her prince? The princess (at least in the old days) would save herself for as long as it took for her one and only husband to be, who would usually be chosen by her parents. She would grow up learning everything there was to be a good wife and mother. When the wedding day arrived, she would dress in white—not because everybody else did—but because it signified her purity.

The same should happen to the woman who fears God. She should spend her life preparing herself for her one and only husband to be, which is God's choice for her. When the day of her wedding arrives, it will definitely be special for her because she will not only be entering into a life-long commitment but also will become one with her prince that same night!

Whenever you feel pressured into having sex with your boyfriend because he pushes it, remember this: it means that he is not the right person for you, because if he were, he would be saving this special occasion when you're both one.

Notes

_____

_____

_____

_____

_____

Alone and Wild

*G*od chose Samson from birth. God sanctified him and his strength was beyond any man of his time. However, Samson didn't agree with living his life for God. He wanted to have fun and be with as many women as he could; after all, he was a strong, handsome young man. He started to play around, as a free wild young man who needed no one in life but his own strength. His end was tragic and shameful. He only achieved victory over his enemies when at the bottom of the pit he realised he needed God after all.

How many young girls think the same way? They want their freedom but not the consequences of it. They want to have fun but not to pay the price for it. Just like a spoiled child who grows up having everything she could possibly need and want, but still is not satisfied. She grows out of her teenage years thinking she's an adult now, but still lives in her parents' house and eats from her parents' table. She wants her independence but lives as her parents' dependent!

God chose Samson and yet He could not do anything to help him because the young man wanted to guide his own life. As a Father, God hates to see us get in trouble but what can He do if we choose to follow our own instincts? Why is God to blame for our own lack of guidance from above?

If you want to be free, by all means—be free. Be free to decide what you want to do in your life, be it good or bad, just don't blame God for what you're going to get because of it. Let's face it, if you're alone out there, you might as well go wild and expect all that comes as a result of your own choices and independent ideas. Forget about God, you chose not to depend on Him.

However, if you're going to ask God for help in achieving anything and I mean ANYTHING in your life, know this: you're placing yourself as God's dependent and therefore you should let Him guide your life. As a dependent of God, you need Him—you know you cannot do it alone and you're tired of trying to.

Usual suspects say, "I want my freedom... I want to do what I feel like doing without anyone telling me what to and not to do... I want to have fun whilst I'm young and free then when I'm older, I'll become a Christian." These are people who are still blinded by this world's temporary fun and then often blame God for every tragic event that happens, be it in their own lives or somewhere1000 miles away.

Come on, let's get real! Either we're independent from God and dependent on our sins or dependent on God and independent from our sins!

"And it shall come to pass in that day that the remnant of Israel, and such as have escaped of the house of Jacob, will never again depend on him who defeated them, but will depend on the LORD, the Holy One of Israel, in truth." (Isa. 10:20)

When you give up your own will in order to depend on God entirely, you can be certain about your future, despite the possible problems that might arise, because you know that God's in control and *"...all things work together for good to those who love God, to those who are the called according to His purpose."* (Rm. 8:28)

Notes

_____

_____

_____

_____

_____

_____

_____

_____

Net or Snare?

There it is, the computer staring at you, practically telling you to turn it on and start browsing the net. Oh, the net, what a vast expanse to be in. A universe of information. Anything you want to see or learn about, just type a couple of words and there you go, it's all there for you. And if you're lonely, it doesn't only give you that option but it also helps you get to know other loners out there—how good is that? What are they up to with this net thing?

If you can picture yourself walking in an unknown town and starting to chat with complete strangers, then you can pretty much envision yourself in Internet meeting sites. In some ways the net can be helpful, but truthfully, it can do more harm than good. People nowadays can't live without it—Isn't that odd? We lived quite comfortably without it just 15 years ago!

It's more often an addiction than anything else. The minute you feel like giving yourself a break, it comes to mind—why not browse the net? Why not check the chat rooms? Why read the Bible when you can browse a multitude of new information? Why pray if you can speak to people across the continent live? And then she wonders why she never grows spiritually, why she's never truly happy. How can she be? She's addicted to the net! Addicted to talking to complete strangers, who most of the time are quite dishonest about who they really are.

Young and sincere women who aspire to be married to a man of God are finding time to invest in chat rooms and networks about all kinds of things. How on earth can they ever be chosen to serve God if they're so involved in the things of this world?

One of the things that helped me the most in getting closer to God was the fact that my life was plain. At that time, I thought my life couldn't be any more boring—no friends, no dating, no fun—just school, home, and church services. I spent most of my time studying, playing with my sister, and reading the Bible. I was criticised a couple of times for not being out there, even by a close relative who at the time thought she was doing me a favour. Nevertheless, I thank God for never, ever being popular and for having had a plain and simple life because that led me straight to God.

I guess most of these young girls and boys who are part of these online networks don't really realise what kind of snare they're getting themselves into. If the devil can get you occupied with anything other than your spiritual life, you'll never grow and mature, and that's the reason why you feel so weak at times. Some are even addicted to sites that are blatantly wrong, and they know it. As much as they want to stop it, they can't—it has become addictive. The more they know, the more they want to find out and the cycle never ends.

Invest in what is good for you. Chat rooms and online networks are more like a deep hole for you to free-fall into. Save yourself from this and invest in the things that can actually lead you to your dreams come true. Read your Bible, pray, commit your life to God, who is the only True Friend you'll ever have anyway. Why look for love and friendship in a world full of deceit and lies called the Internet? I'm sure you're worth much more than that!

Notes

_____

_____

_____

_____

_____

_____

_____

Why She's a Loser

ot because she didn't have any dreams—she did have them, as a matter of fact, many of them. And at some point, she even worked towards them, but because of so many distractions that surrounded her, she lost her will and all her dreams went down the drain. Today, she's a loser, though she won't admit it. She often thinks she's on top of her world, with all the beauty she's got, all the attention and all the eyes on her. But there are times that only she knows about, when she feels empty, sad, as if nothing in the world is worth pursuing.

This is the life of many young people. They're so full of potential and talents, one would think they had it all to succeed with God by their side. But in fact, the latter is still not present. God is not who they hold by their side. The only thing by their side is the world and its attractions. Fun is all they want and all they pursue. Their time is filled with all the things that add nothing to their spiritual life: parties, movies, music, Internet, video games and dating.

It may be harsh to say "she's a loser" just now, but think about it—if your time is filled with vain things for most of your 24 hours, what can you say about yourself? Do you really think you're on your way to success?

Success is an achievement. Achievements can only be conquered—they're not dropped on your lap! Much of what we are comes from what we were and what we did, and if what we were and did was vain, it is to expect that all that is left for us is an empty, discontent life.

"Rejoice, O young man, in your youth, and let your heart cheer you in the days of your youth; walk in the ways of your heart, and in the sight of your eyes; but know that for all these God will bring

you into judgment. Therefore remove sorrow from your heart, and put away evil from your flesh, for childhood and youth are vanity. Remember now your Creator in the days of your youth, before the difficult days come, and the years draw near when you say, 'I have no pleasure in them." (Ec. 11:9 - 10; 12:1)

Youth is preparation for adult life, much like a school, so that you may learn what is good or not good to pursue for the rest of your life. If you think like most young people, you'll use your youth to pursue fun, and then later when you're grown, you'll be like many adults—depressed, alone, ashamed of their past, a feeling like they wasted a lifetime.

Rejoice, now that you're young and you can learn easily; now that you can make a good beginning so that the middle and end of your life can reap all its good fruits; now that you can plan ahead wisely and not waste time and energy on what won't add anything to your life. Rejoice in your youth, invest in your spiritual life, prepare yourself for your future, when difficulties come, prepare yourself for a relationship that will last a lifetime. There's so much to invest in now, early in life, so much to achieve for the rest of your life—why waste it? Think about it. But if you still decide on wasting it, just remember to blame all your future failures entirely on yourself, for you decided to go the way of the crowd—taking it easy and having that temporary "fun".

Notes

_____

_____

_____

_____

_____

_____

_____

_____

_____

Ugly Me?

$\mathcal{I}$ was taking the train one day and couldn't help but notice this young girl seated in front of me. Her hair, her nails, as well as her whole outfit were black, though she was white as snow and her hair roots revealed her light natural hair. Many people looked at her also, then looked away because of the rebellious way she dressed, which was probably what she expected from people anyway. To me, she was a beautiful young woman who just didn't know how beautiful and full of potential she was.

But isn't that the way many women think? They look at themselves in the mirror and wonder why they don't look as beautiful as so and so; they dislike their appearance, their walk, their voice, their body shape, their hair, their personality, and so on. And that is how they dress themselves—the "couldn't care less" way!

There's something really wrong with this behaviour. You'll read about it in books and hear about it in self-improvement conferences, but the truth is that knowledge alone does not change a thing. People know they have to love themselves in order to live a more fulfilled life but they can't, though they want to. That is because there is an ongoing inner battle inside of them between truth and lie.

How can anyone allow a lie to overcome the truth? As hard as it seems, we all do it. Every time we believe in the thought that says we're not good enough, we believe in a lie. If you question that thought, you'll realise that it doesn't make sense. Why am I not good enough? Because I didn't do my job as well as someone else? Why am I ugly? Because of my feet? Why am I inferior to my friend? Because of my educational background? No way!

The truth says that we are only inferior, ugly, and not good enough if we want to be. We are not these things because of what we have or don't have, or of what we are and are not, but solely because we think that way about ourselves. Why then believe in a lie? Maybe someone close said something that has marked your self-image to this day, but question what he or she said. What is the basis of what was said? Is that a fact or just thoughtless words? Probably the latter.

If you question these evil ideas about yourself every time, you'll soon notice how silly and foolish you were to believe them in the first place. And then you'll be able to love yourself as you deserve. Just look around you and you'll see that there's no one like you. No one in millions and billions of people! Your body may need some improvements but that is just because you were not taking proper care of it. Once you start caring for it and loving it enough to invest in it, you'll start seeing its true beauty.

One can only take good care of what they like. If you love yourself, you'll take good care of yourself. You'll take good care of your health, your body, your looks, and even the house you live in. Once you can look in the mirror and like what you see, people who look at you will also like what they see because... *"As a man thinks in his heart, so is he."* (Pv. 23.7)

Notes

_____

_____

_____

_____

_____

_____

_____

_____

_____

_____

The Woman in You

Over the years the concept of women, what we mean, and what we can do in this world has changed so much that it scares me. Many men started looking at women in a different way as if their whole purpose in life was to be a mere object of temporary use, while it was good and young.

Not too long ago, women were looked at with respect and honour. Women were approached with reverence and discretion and it was an honour for a man to marry a lady. Nowadays, most men couldn't care less if a woman is standing in the bus or carrying loads of bags. Many will leave their wives still pregnant and in need of their help to live with another woman, as if she is of no use anymore.

That is not what God had in mind when He created Eve. He made her out of Adam's own body as if saying, she is your own body—take good care of her as you take good care of your own body. She was taken from his side and not from his feet or from his head, as if saying, she is to be your companion and not your floor mat or your boss. He made her suitable for him because he needed a helper. If Adam could have done it alone, God wouldn't have taken the trouble of creating her.

The woman God created was someone a man would live eternally with, who would be his helper and best friend. He created her beautiful and lovely, an understanding and merciful being, who with only a kiss would melt in her man's arms and forget their misunderstanding. An incredible being whose gentleness and warmth is beyond anything in this world—if only she knew the woman inside herself!

The problem is that women in general do not know how special they have been created, so they go and tear their image and degrade themselves with whatever they can find in order to attract a man. They will do anything, whatever it takes, no matter how, only to become an attraction to men.

The tighter their clothes are, the bigger their breasts are, the more seductive they look, the less clothes they wear, the louder they speak or laugh, the more men they are seen with, the more sexy they talk or dress... They think this way they can get the men of their dreams, but how wrong they are. They are nowhere near to getting a man who will honour and respect them.

Men were created as conquerors and anything that is too easily won is just not worth getting. The harder it is for him to win a woman, the more he wants her. The less he sees of her body, the more he will conclude how attractive she might be. The more reserved she seems to be, the more interesting he finds her.

Think with me—if looks and looking sexy are what it takes, why are some many of these beautiful, body toned, sexy stars so unfortunate in their love lives? They have money, they have the looks, they have the career, they have the popularity, they have the right connections, and yet many of them have no permanent husband!

In talking about women, the One who specialised in how she was meant to be suggests the following:

"...Rather let it be the hidden person of the heart, with the incorruptible beauty of a gentle and quiet spirit, which is very precious in the sight of God." (1 Pe. 3:4) And in Proverbs 11:22, it says, *"As a ring of gold in a swine's snout, so is a lovely woman who lacks discretion."*

Now it is a matter of you wanting to find this woman in you or not!

Notes

_____

_____

_____

_____

The Temple of Beauty

Women are truly beautiful in so many ways. Our shape is unique and though we try to hide it at times and even lose a bit here and there, we wouldn't be women if it weren't for our curves. Then there are the extra features that men simply can't get enough of—the soft lips, the smooth skin, the delicate hands and feet, and those angel eyes.

I think that many of us don't realise how beautiful we are. Most colours look great on us. If we wear our hair up or down, long or short, we still turn heads. And clothes, oh my—we look great in them.

Basically, we don't need to be Beyoncé to be admired. We have all that it takes and that is why we don't need to show more than what's easily apparent when we dress discreetly.

Our beauty can sometimes be a snare of the devil to men. There have been men who stopped following God because of such distractions. Our bodies should not be tools to destroy a man's conscience before God.

Our body is the temple of the Holy Spirit, so says the Word of God. We must take good care of it and use it for God's glory and not shame. I understand that sometimes it is hard to tell what's good and not good to wear; after all, there is always a new fashion out there and when we are not part of it, we feel old-fashioned and even a bit degraded by other women. Believe me, I've been there.

And sometimes, it's not that the clothes are tight; it's the weight we gained on those usual areas. It's hard, I know, but we still need to think about what a simple tight pair of jeans can do to a man's imagination. Why allow the beauty that God gave us to work against Him?

Instead of dressing provocatively, let's be wise and dress for success—the kind of success that gives God the glory and us the respect.

"...Whoever looks at a woman to lust for her has already committed adultery with her in his heart." (Mt. 5:28)

"Therefore, if food makes my brother stumble, I will never again eat meat, lest I make my brother stumble." (I Cor. 8:13) (Although the apostle is talking about food here, the principle is the same).

"...A seductress is a narrow well." (Pv. 23:27)

Notes

Marilyn Monroes

$\mathcal{S}$he was having a hard time coming down the stairs at the school's entrance. There were just too many books to be carried, plus the mini-skirt and the high, high heels just made it harder for her. In a split second, she fell and all those hours spent in front of the mirror earlier that morning were out the window. Her top had almost gone completely and her mini was covering for her top. She thought she could actually hear passersby thinking how ridiculous she looked.

Have you ever thought of how we women are generally taken for granted? Women used to be praised and respected. Men used to take off their hats or stand up simply out of courtesy at a woman's arrival. The idea of heavy labour was just out of the question for us ladies.

Nowadays, we have to beg for a kind soul to give us a hand. Often, we're the ones to ride a bus standing up because most men just don't see the point of expressing any respect for us. Some women are beaten up just because of something they said, whilst in the past, to beat up a woman was just something unheard of.

Why has the value of women been lost with time? What triggered this huge change of attitude from men's point of view? The truth is shameful but necessary to be written about, to be taught by mothers, to be explained in schools, and moreover, to be grasped no matter how hard it is to swallow: We women are the cause of our own devaluation. We gave birth to this whole scenario.

It all began with the idea that we were too beautiful to be hidden behind clothes. Our shape and beauty made old and young men happy. The more they saw, the more they wanted to see. The fewer clothes we wore, the more beautiful we looked. All eyes and attention started to be focused on us and who's the woman that does not enjoy that? That's what we've always craved all our lives: attention, praise, recognition, to be found beautiful, to be a princess, and have it all.

Marilyn Monroe became a star out of that idea. She couldn't act or sing, but she became a star only from the fact that she was willing to show more than most women would in her time. Men adored her, women envied her, the press said she had it all, and singers wrote songs about her. But still her end was a sad one. She must have been the saddest woman alive in those days for she had given all she had and all she got in return was a feeling of being used throughout her life.

She was used, misused, and used again. All she wanted was attention, someone who would love her, and indeed that is what she got, but the attention was merely because of her body and the love was merely because of what she stood for.

There are still plenty of Marilyn Monroes nowadays, trying all they can to become this famous and perfect woman at any price. But is this fame and popularity really worth exposing yourself to others? Is fashion really giving our womanhood a boost or just degrading us altogether?

Notes

The First Impression

What is the first thing you see in another woman? Her attitudes? The way she speaks? The way she walks? Probably, if you really think about it, the first thing you see is the way she dresses—her hair, her clothes, her make up, and her whole outfit. I know it's shallow to do it but isn't it what usually happens? Before getting to know someone, it is their appearance we see. Now, what first impression is your appearance making on people you meet?

You may say, "Beauty comes from within" and you are completely right. But inner beauty doesn't mean your appearance is not important! When you like yourself, you take good care of your body and appearance. It has nothing to do with vanity, which is an extreme way of caring more for your appearance than anything else in life. Vanity is wrong but loving yourself to the point of always making sure you are looking your best—be it for your husband or for yourself—that my friend, is inner beauty coming out!

So many young women of God waste opportunities of winning the man of their dreams because they think this fact is not important. They are always so busy at work or with other matters in life and so there's no time to put on some make up or wear something special each day. Think with me, how else will he like you if your exterior does not reflect your interior? He doesn't know you yet to like you for who you are, how can you expect him to like you "by faith"? Let's use our intelligent faith!

Other women allow their husbands to drift away when seeing other beautiful women because they think that after marriage, looks are not important anymore. They are practically paving the way for their husband's infidelity! Getting married is just the first step—staying married is the final and hardest step which many people haven't been able to achieve. Therefore, after marriage is when you must look better still. Your husband is a man, remember that. And if we women look at other beautiful women, imagine men! Your husband must be able to think, "Why would I settle for a Beetle, if I have a Mercedes at home?" Get it?

Are you growing older? Don't let your age hide your beauty. As you grow old, let your beauty grow as well, You don't need any surgery or makeovers as seen on TV, all you need is a bit of creativity and courage to be a little adventurous with your looks. You only look old when you want to, though the lines may show by the day, you don't have to stop looking nice because of them.

The first impression you give to anyone is the way you look. Why would you not care and improve your looks? The way you look will say many things about you such as if you are into details (accessories), fun (bright colours), secure about yourself (skirts), young in spirit (in fashion), adventurous (new hairstyles), decorative (make-up), and so on. Take the time to improve your looks and you'll see how your children will admire you, your husband will only have eyes for you, your friends will follow you around, and strangers will wonder what's so special about you!

Notes

_____

_____

_____

_____

_____

_____

_____

_____

_____

_____

Dressed For a Downfall

It was a lovely Saturday and so I decided to take my son to the park. To my shock there she was, among so many children and families, a mother wearing only a black-laced bra as her top. She didn't care that there were hundreds of children around playing and actually, the children didn't care either. No one but me looked shocked!

It is incredible how the majority of young children already know how the opposite sex looks. Children nowadays are different, more mature in many ways, and it is even scary. "Where did their innocence go?" I wonder, but then I remember common sense left our society even before innocence did. Why does it seem that bad things are acceptable and good for all, and good things are outdated and not important anymore?

Think with me. One of the most ordinary scenes nowadays is to see naked or half-naked women. They are everywhere—in movies' love scenes, getting a tan in the park, advertising soap on a billboard, making their way down the catwalk, and even going to church. Honestly speaking, I don't think they realise they're naked at all, because the majority of women nowadays do the same! In order for a woman to wear decent clothes, she cannot even think about buying her size, for it will surely look tight, uncomfortable, too low, and indiscreet.

In the name of fashion, career, and even age, women expose their most intimate parts for all to see. Clothes are now made to show instead of hide. Fabrics now are the ones we used to wear for underwear. Dresses look more and more like lingerie and meant to be worn without any underwear.

I remember the time when underwear was one of the things we hid the most. It was shameful for anyone to know EVEN the colour of the underwear we used; nowadays, underwear is to be shown off and exposed. And some of them are so small and insignificant that I wonder what's the purpose. Bras used to be worn for protection. Nowadays, they're for cleavage. The tighter the trousers, the better they look, or so women say. What's going on?

Men used to make a big deal about it at first, but now it's all too common, overused, and ordinary. They got tired of seeing so much of what is not supposed to be seen. Many don't even look anymore, others make fun, and some look down on women altogether.

It seems it's all part of some evil plan to degrade women. Some fashion styles have led women to their downfall. It seems the goal is to lower their value before men, so they consequently would not want to enter into any commitment with them, but just use them for their own pleasures. And with this, causing more and more dysfunctional families, with no father, no husband, and no morals.

Why give this world the satisfaction? Why let your body, which is the temple of the Holy Spirit, be the centre of the wrong kind of attention? Why be the cause of so many men falling into sin?

Let's dress for success and not for a downfall!

Women are truly beautiful in so many ways. Our shape is unique to us only and our features are so delicate and perfect. Our beauty can be seen without us baring our bodies naked. Let's use what we have to bring us good and not harm, lift us up and not push down. Let's dress for success!

We don't need to be old-fashioned to dress properly. All we need is the right goal in mind. When the goal is to grab everybody's attention, it won't bring us success and all we'll get is the wrong kind of attention.

Our goal in dressing ourselves shouldn't be to attract everybody's attention to ourselves or create the wrong image of who we really are. Our goal should be one that will bring respect, and a good and positive impression. Unfortunately, we can't always count on fashion to do that for us. There are good and bad fashion choices and we must be able to recognise which is which. Use your conscience and you'll know what to wear.

Notes

_____
_____
_____
_____
_____
_____
_____
_____
_____
_____
_____
_____
_____
_____
_____
_____
_____
_____
_____
_____
_____
_____

Your Life

eing young and looking beautiful is one of the top priorities for girls nowadays. And after that, of course, boys. They think about the here and now, how beautiful they should look, how popular they should be, how much fun they're having because of their age, and which boy to go out with and perhaps be the first to show them what sex is all about.

Schools are more like vehicles to get the above easily, instead of safeguards to avoid them. And so parents lose control of their young girls. They cannot tell or know what is going on with them. Many girls come from school and go straight to their bedroom. How can a parent know or make him/herself available to help? And if the mother calls for a chat, the young girl quickly shows her long face, turning the mother's hopes down.

I've been there. These thoughts came to my mind years ago when I was in school. There is pressure having these thoughts everyday in school, among friends, and even sometimes at home. Young women are pressured into thinking about the here and now while young men, though they do think about the present quite often, are usually more pressured to think about their future.

I remember when I was a teenager being very close to my mother and often being misunderstood and criticised by the other girls in school. All their criticism didn't bother me because I had no reason to ignore or avoid my mother, why would I do that now? It shocked me the way they spoke about their parents. They obviously did not respect them at all, saying how they hated their parents, how they wished they had different parents, how disgusting it was to see their parents kissing each other, and how they longed to leave their house.

It didn't make sense at all and yet this is one of the most common reactions from teenage girls in recent time. It shows how unaware they are of things that really matter. And it's not unusual for their own children later on to think the same way about them, as the cycle continues through time.

And this is the reason why so many young girls start having a "family", which consists of only her and a child. They were only thinking about the here and now.

Are you young and free? Use that to your advantage. Take your life seriously, after all, it's not a game or a soap opera—it's reality! Whatever you do today will reflect on your life tomorrow. Love your parents. After all the work they've been through to raise you up, that's the least you can give back to them. Love your body. Don't waste it with mediocre sexual experiences, wait for the day when you'll become one with the man that will be yours for life. Love your future. Work towards it, study as much as you can, and be the best you can be!

Notes

Oh, That Love Life!

$\mathcal{I}$sn't it a pain sometimes? You want to focus on other things but the heart keeps on asking for love, for a companion, for some kind of relationship. You try to fill your day with activities and work, but still, when night comes, so does the thought, and suddenly, you're dreaming away in some place that may not even exist walking along with a man who loves you.

As much as we want to think we don't need it, we do—we know how much we do. It's not that we can't live without it, but it's more like how much happier we would be with it. Our love life is extremely important, and though you may be a woman with your own personal goals in life, how much easier would it be if at the end of a busy day you could go home to someone?

It is a proven fact that we crave for fulfilment in this area of life, which is something God must have built in us since the beginning of time. He saw how Adam's life would be much better if he had a helper—a woman. Mind you that Adam had everything any man could possibly want. He was rich in every way and in control of everything that existed in those times, but still, God saw his need.

God still sees this need today and wants to make matches that will last a lifetime, but even so, He has met some resistance from us. He knows what's best for everyone, and yet not everyone wants to get what He has to offer. And so they go choosing whomever they "feel" most attracted to, forcing their way into a match that was never meant to be.

Young women who are afraid of staying alone for the rest of their lives begin to rush into any relationship that comes their way. Older women who can't stand loneliness and insecurity any longer give themselves to a "commitment-to-be" relationship that only brings them more heartache. And the cycle keeps on going round and round. When does it end? When will God ever intervene for them?

When they finally give up trying to do what they can't, God will then be able to become their ultimate matchmaker. And when you think about it, it makes perfect sense. He's God and therefore knows who is who from the inside out, making Him the perfect matchmaker of all time. He makes no mistakes—ever.

Your love life is important and by all means, you must give it time, but don't take the place of God in choosing who is right for you. If you only put this area in His Hands and use your faith by trusting in Him and not let your doubts annul your faith, God will provide. He always provides. For God, it doesn't matter if you're young, old, or getting old. It doesn't matter if you're a widow or a divorcée. All that matters is that you trust Him and do from now on what only you can do: Pray and act your faith.

Notes

Not Your All

$\mathcal{S}$he loved him so much that words simply could not express it. And so she gave him her all. Everything in her life revolved around him, the love of her life, until the day she finally realised that she was not the one he looked forward to seeing everyday. His time and efforts were not focused on her anymore and the ground opened under her as she fell into a deep pit. Darkness seemed constant and loneliness was all she wanted. Her friends and loved ones tried to pull her out of it, but she insisted on staying in and never having to face another day.

Women who give their all to a relationship are always in danger of going through the above. It is not because relationships aren't good enough or trustworthy, but because men, children, relatives, and friends are humans, and humans make mistakes. Disappointment is inevitable when you're dealing with someone else, whoever they may be. The minute you start expecting perfection or too much from someone else, you immediately put yourself in a vulnerable place—a place where you will eventually get hurt.

It is vital that you give your best to a relationship you believe in, but your best should never be your whole self—to the point that if anything happens to that relationship, you also lose yourself. You have got to love yourself better than that and have some kind of self-protection so that you can never be pulled down if things around you go downhill.

So how much of yourself should you give in a relationship? Simply your best. Your best is not your all; your best is a big part of you, but not all of you. Your all can only be given when you are sure it will be safe and secure, and that only God is worthy of. We know that God will never disappoint us. Things may not happen at the time we want, nevertheless He has a reason, and He has His time. He is the Only One who deserves our all.

It is sad to see so many women giving their all to men, children, parents, relatives, and friends and just part of themselves to God. They just don't understand how much wrong they are doing to themselves. They are setting a trap for them to fall into. Some think that it's hard to give their all to God after all, they have never seen Him. So I ask, who gave you the strength to wake up that morning when you had spent the whole night crying? Or who understands you when nobody does? Or even, who was there next to you when loneliness overwhelmed you? Do you think you've gone through these things all alone? Think again! Do you still not see Him?

People will often break your heart and that is life—either you protect yourself or suffer the consequences. Wise women protect themselves and give their all to the One they can truly rely on whatever the circumstances. There are few women who truly understand this important concept of life and interestingly enough, it's these women that are the most sought after.

Notes

_____

_____

_____

_____

_____

_____

_____

_____

_____

_____

_____

Prince Charming

Ever since I was a little girl in my father's house, I dreamed of marrying a "prince charming" and raising a family with him. I remember writing on a piece of paper all the qualities I wanted my prince to have and with total faith in my heart, I left it in God's hands.

I specifically asked that my first boyfriend would be my husband for the rest of my life. At the time, I was only 10 years old. It is a shame that I didn't keep that little piece of paper, so I could enjoy reading it today, as I praise God for answering it as well as giving me even more.

As I grew up, people started to wonder when I would start dating. They would introduce me to someone here and another there, but I remained firm with my decision to have only one boyfriend who would eventually be my husband. I wasn't on the same wavelength as my friends at school. The more boyfriends they had, the more popular they became. I was considered an "alien" because of my principle, but I didn't mind because I had an assurance in my heart that God had someone special for me.

And so it was; I met my husband when I was 16 years old and he became my first boyfriend. We had everything in common and the more we got to know each other, the more we were certain that we were made for each other. We had the same vision, same spirit, same desires, and same faith.

It didn't take long for us to get married and start our journey together. Our wedding day was the happiest day of our lives after knowing the Lord Jesus.

If I had to do it all over again, I would, because marrying a man of God is like signing a lifelong commitment of happiness. We overcome all our battles together. It does not matter where we go or live; we are one and simply cannot live apart.

This is the testimony of my life to show to you that no matter how many broken marriages are out there or how high the divorce rate is, God blessed me—not because I was special but because I used my faith in Him and stood by it until the end.

We have been married for over 16 years now and we love each other more and more with each year that passes by. It is like being on permanent honeymoon! We laugh together, we cry together, we play together, we overcome together—we're a team! Nothing and no one can separate us because God is our bond.

As surely as God lives, He wants you to have a blessed marriage and family. He created it and it is His plan for every human being. The problem is, that human beings today do not want God interfering with their lives. They want independence, "freedom". If only they knew how prone to failure and suffering they are, without God by their side...

Back at school, some of those popular girls who had loads and loads of fun and boyfriends are today either alone or divorced. People turn to drugs, alcohol, gambling, and head down all the wrong ways because of the lack of having a family, a true family of God.

Be wise and seek God for a real family, a real marriage and you will know what true happiness is all about.

Notes

_____

_____

_____

_____

_____

_____

_____

_____

The Man of God

His love for God is so intense and true that he would never do anything to hurt or bring Him to shame. He fears God and that makes him faithful to Him, to his wife, and those around him.

His faithfulness, his character, his wisdom, and his understanding make him stand out from all other men. He can't be found just anywhere. Such men are very hard to find.

This outstanding man is not a super model or a body builder. His appearance doesn't really matter once you meet him. He speaks wisely as if he has lived years ahead. His conversation is constructive and makes one pleased to talk to him.

He fears nothing, not because he thinks he's on the top of the world, but because he knows he can count on the Holy Spirit at all times. Nothing comes easy for him but he takes on every challenge and by faith, he overcomes them all. He inspires others and through him, God is glorified.

He's truly prince charming. The woman who marries him will have his love and faithfulness for the rest of her life. He'll teach and listen to her. And having it all, he'll still play and have fun, but she'll always be included in it. He'll be pleased when she's around, even when she's just sitting by his side. Just being there is enough to make him happy... He's doesn't ask for much—only that she gives him her best as he'll give her his best.

He's hard working. He won't rest until he gets what he wants. He's never taking it easy, but his goal is always to achieve and conquer something that will honour God. He's serious about the things that are important in life and he won't take failures home. He's sure of himself and needs no one. He has it all except the one thing that makes him complete: a wife.

Yes, he's every woman's dream come true and yet, he's looking for a wife! Some even think this description is way too much and too good to be true, but that's because they were unfortunate to have never met a man like him.

This man is not recognised in the world—people who are jealous of his righteous way of thinking actually make fun of him. Women, who don't have a clue about his qualities, reject him thinking that he's from outer space because he can never be found in pubs or nightclubs. It's an amazing phenomenon for them to see him react to their seductive words and moves by simply turning away.

He's not attracted to women like most men are, another way that makes him so different from the others. He's not looking for a girl-friend just to have fun. He's looking for a wife.

"Who is like a wise man? A man's wisdom makes his face shine, and the sternness of his face is changed." (Ecl. 8:1)

Notes

_____

_____

_____

_____

_____

_____

_____

_____

_____

_____

_____

_____

_____

How to Attract a Man of God

Almost every young girl in the church is looking for a man of God, and yet only a few know how to attract one. Many do not understand why he is not attentive to their looks. They take so long to get dressed to come to church and the man of God doesn't even know they exist. So they try to approach him and make their move, but he seems indifferent to them as if he were from another planet.

She will not catch his attention by the way she dresses or walks, or by the friends she has, because he is just not like every other guy. Appearance and flirtatious moves don't really catch his eye. The man of God is a rare precious stone and so is the woman he is looking for. Whilst every man is looking for a beautiful girl, a man of God is looking for a woman of God.

This woman of God is not religious or a saint by any means. She is human and despite all her mistakes and shortcomings, she fears God, and for that reason she tries to serve Him as much as possible. In every spare moment, she's doing something to serve God. It's just the way she is—serving God is what makes her happy.

She is seen doing the things nobody likes doing. Her coming to the church is never to attract anyone's attention but God's. She makes herself available even though she still has many commitments of her own in her studies and work—but these are always secondary to her because what she really wants is to serve God.

So the man of God starts seeing her dedication and wonders who she is. Is this the one? Does she have the same goals as he? But he will not get to know her just yet—there is still much to be seen before he makes an approach.

He then starts getting information about her—if she is younger than he is and will respect him, if she is mature enough to become his wife soon, if she is responsible at home so she can take good care of his home, if she is naturally submissive to her parents so she can submit to him, if she is respectful in her work place so she will be respectful at home, if she is a true servant in the church so she can truly serve him, and if she is faithful to God so she can be faithful to him as her husband.

If all he finds out about her is positive, he gets the assurance from God that she is the one. There is no more need to pray about it, and so he approaches her and lets his new feelings and assurance towards her be known.

That is how a man of God is attracted. He is not looking for a perfect woman—just one who serves God.

Notes

_____

_____

_____

_____

_____

_____

_____

_____

_____

_____

_____

_____

_____

_____

_____

_____

People Who Deserve to be Single

"Beautiful, 31-year-old woman looking for a romantic and sophisticated man of God who loves walks on the beach and watching old romantic movies; who's willing to commit to a lifetime partner and have children. He must be this size, have these looks, be this age, of this culture, have this personality, and have this goal."

In short, he's got to be perfect and rare. How many of those who are happily married can say they've found the perfect man? Honestly speaking, none. Humans can never be perfect. Perfection is only possible in romantic movies and books, where everything is imagined by the author.

Women who think there's a perfect man out there for them are not being realistic at all. They confuse a perfect man with a perfect match, which is something else entirely. A perfect match is someone who fits as your other half; he's not necessarily perfect, and should definitely not be like you. He must be different in many ways in order to match with you.

My husband and I are very different from one another and yet we match. It's not about perfection at all. When I first laid eyes on my husband, I tell you, he was everything I wanted—a man of God. Of course his looks did attract me at first, but that wasn't the sole purpose I chose him. He had the necessary characteristics to make me happy. I wasn't worried if he was romantic or not, or if his personality was like so and so. He was in fact, very serious and possibly shy from afar, not as bold as I thought my first boyfriend would be. Nevertheless, when push came to shove, I saw his boldness in what really mattered and that caught me.

Some single women tend to be difficult and choosy, as if they were perfect themselves. Wise women know that in this day and age, the few men of God available are precious. They know that they can easily learn to adjust to some of their imperfections, after all, they have them too and they'll need a man to adjust to them one day.

For this reason, the title of this article, though rude and inconsiderate, is unfortunately true. People who won't settle for anything less than what they expect in life, miss great blessings that come in disguise. Give the guy a chance! Who knows, he may be a blessing that you're tossing away because he just doesn't have what so and so has.

Besides, if you get a boyfriend that is everything you wanted, how will you ever make a difference in marrying him? If he's so perfect, it's probably better for him to stay alone and single just the way he is. Marrying someone is not only about committing to him for the rest of your life but also about adding to his life, being a suitable helper that will truly make a difference.

Remember Rebecca? She hadn't yet met Isaac but believed that God was the One choosing her, and so she took a great step of faith in leaving her family behind to meet a stranger who feared God. When Isaac met her for the first time, God got to work. First they took a step of faith and then God took care of the rest. Read about her story in Genesis 24.

Notes

_____

_____

_____

_____

_____

_____

_____

_____

_____

_____

Falling in Love

*Y*our heart beats faster and faster every time you see him. You look at his eyes and they seem to pierce deep into yours and you feel shy instantly as if he could read what you were thinking. Your feelings for this man of your dreams are so powerful that you fear what you're capable of doing just to have him all for yourself. You've fallen in love and there's nothing and no one that can change that.

I've always asked myself why the expression "to fall in love" sounds so negative, as if you were actually falling because of something so pure and beautiful. God is the One who created love and I am positively certain that He never meant it to be something negative or something that would make people do crazy things because of it. Nevertheless people do it everyday. Women leave their faith in God because of the "love of their life" everyday and everywhere.

What is real love then? Certainly, the term "falling in love" does not really describe it, if so, women wouldn't suffer so much heartache in this world because of it. In 1 Corinthians 13:1-8, God answers that through the apostle Paul:

"Though I speak with the tongues of men and of angels, but have not love, I have become sounding brass or a clanging cymbal. And though I have the gift of prophecy, and understand all mysteries and all knowledge, and though I have all faith, so that I could remove mountains, but have not love, I am nothing. And though I bestow all my goods to feed the poor, and though I give my body to be burned, but have not love, it profits me nothing. Love suffers long and is kind; love does not envy; love does not parade itself, is not puffed up; does not behave rudely, does not seek its own, is not provoked, thinks no evil; does not rejoice in iniquity, but rejoices in the truth; bears all things, believes all things, hopes all things, endures all things. Love never fails."

Love never fails. How can people fall in love then? The truth is that "falling in love" doesn't really mean having this love, the love that God has created and shown with His Own life. If you read the verses above carefully, meditating on each word, you'll realise that love is an entirely different attitude than what this world teaches us through songs, heartaches, and misfortunes. It's pure and it's meant to be perfect, unfailing, and unconditional.

In light of this, the term "falling in love" can only mean "falling into trouble". So many give up their all because of this fake love that ends up destroying the only hope they had—true love hopes all things. Some women go to the extent of getting pregnant so that their lover will not leave. But true love does not seek its own and is not provoked. Others go to bed with their boyfriends to show how much they love them. But true love does not rejoice in iniquity neither does it parade itself.

What have you called love? Perhaps that is why you feel so disoriented about it. You've been letting yourself "fall in love" whilst true love has never ever crossed your path, and as long as you keep allowing yourself to fall, it will never come. Stop this nonsense, clean your mind, and turn to the one True Love, our Lord Jesus Christ, and He'll show you all the wonders that come with it.

Notes

Lonely No More

"I can't stand the loneliness," she said with tears in her eyes whilst looking at her trembling hands. "It's one thing to believe in God and live a life of sacrifice, but to live it alone is just too much to bear! When will God ever bless me with a husband, a man that will fill this gap in my life?" This woman came to me for counselling on a Friday evening and though I could see where she was coming from, there was no way I could answer that question for her.

There are questions we Christians ask that are entirely ours to answer—no one besides you can really know why things are not happening in your life, because it's your life and it can't get any more personal than that. However, many single Christian women face the same problem in their love life. They feel as though their Christianity has made them lonely and frustrated, as if that is the price they have to pay for being women of God.

We know very well that the minute we start doing things the way we think is best, we fail and it's not because God is up there trying to make it hard for us or playing with our feelings in a game trivial, but it's due to that old rule of life—you reap what you sow. How many failed relationships have you had before knowing God? Based on this fact, you could easily conclude that the source of your loneliness is not in your Christianity.

Picture this: God, who has tried so many times to come near you, has finally succeeded. But now He faces another obstacle since you're always thinking about your future and about the life you've always dreamed of. You hardly ever come to Him to get to know Him better, instead, you're always asking Him this and that and when things don't happen in the time and way you want, you're mad at Him. He loves you so much but it's so hard to see you wanting someone or something else above Him that it just hurts. He knows that time will teach you a lesson but when are you ever going to learn that lesson?

The Bible says that God is a jealous God (read Deuteronomy 4.24; Exodus 25:5; 34:14; Joshua 24:19; Ezekiel 39:25; Nahum 1:2) and that He *"...is your Husband, The LORD of hosts is His name; and your Redeemer is the Holy One of Israel; He is called the God of the whole earth."* (Isa. 54:5)

God wants to bless and make you the happiest woman in the world. After all, isn't that what you want for someone you love? The problem is that you have put Him aside and allowed your anxieties to take over. He's no longer your first love but Someone who needs to prove His love for you by giving you "stuff". It's funny how ridiculous that sounds but that's exactly what often happens.

Be wise and trust in God for all your needs. Don't let them be the cause of your biggest loss of all—the One Husband who will never fail or disappoint you!

Notes

_____

_____

_____

_____

_____

_____

_____

_____

_____

_____

_____

_____

_____

Christian Dating: The Dos & Don'ts

It's not uncommon for Christians to feel uneasy when it comes to dating, after all the world makes it sound so easy and simple. Everything is allowed as long as you feel comfortable doing it, they say. The truth is that dating can either be a blessing or a curse to a Christian. Many have fallen into sin and many others became stronger in their faith all because of the dos and don'ts in Christian dating. Every Christian should be aware of these so they may never jeopardise their everlasting status before God.

The first thing one must know about dating is that it's not necessarily about going out and having fun. It's much more than what you would do with friends and relatives. It's the time you take in order to know the person you are dating and vice-versa. You are both strangers, even if you've known each other for years. You don't really know each other well enough in order to commit your entire life into marriage, and so you date—you find out as much as possible about each other.

Christian dating is like Christian living—they're both very different from the world. If a Christian wants to date like she used to date in the world, she will evidently fall into sin and consequently feel far from God. Wise Christians know that their salvation is more important than anything in this world and therefore should not be taken for granted because of fleshly and temporary desires. That is why it's important that you protect yourself from falling by taking precautions such as:

1.   Always date in public and never late at night—because it makes it harder for you to give in to your fleshly desires. There will be so many people around that it will be almost impossible for you to do anything you will regret later. It will help you do only what you're really supposed to be doing: talking!

2. Always wear discreet and appropriate clothes—because your body is already very tempting for the guy you are dating and if you are letting more than what is enough show, it will be very hard for him to resist temptation. I remember that my mother taught me this right when I started dating. I stopped wearing clothes I loved wearing just so that I wouldn't be the stumbling block in my boyfriend's conscience.

3. Avoid going to each other's house when there's no one there—because it will be very tempting to get physical and consequently fall into sin. If you have to go, avoid kissing and even hugging each other whilst there—temptation will be strong!

4. When hugging each other, avoid touching or pressing against each other's intimate parts of the body. This way, you will protect yourselves from temptation.

Remember, dating is not about touching and having fun—it's about knowing each other well so that you may decide if this is the person you want to spend the rest of your life with. Christians don't date just for fun because they know deep inside that this kind of dating only hurts later on. Christians date to find the one and only partner for life.

Notes

_____

_____

_____

_____

_____

_____

_____

_____

_____

_____

_____

_____

When to Move On

*H*e told you he needs some time to think. He left the house and you simply don't know where he is or whom he's with. He said he loves you but wants to keep things as they are. It's getting harder to wake up in the morning, time seems to stand still, and you feel confused and clueless about what to do next. You're stuck.

But everything in life moves forward—people and animals are being born and dying everyday, trees and flowers are flourishing and withering everyday, the sun and the moon are rising and setting everyday, and you are growing older everyday. You look out your window and everything seems to be still but the truth is that many things are happening right at that moment and it only seems still from a distance.

You may think that you are also taking your time to think and come to a conclusion on what you'll be doing next, but remember that time is not standing still. Time is not waiting for you to decide what to do. It's moving on and so is everybody and everything else around you. Standing still will obviously take you nowhere and could even prevent you from achieving better things in life.

Why should you wait anyway? Aren't you wasting your precious time? Maybe you think that if you move on, you'll never have this person in your life again, but if so, does that mean you'll never find someone better than him? If he's as great as you say he is, then why has he left you? Why does he need more time?

The time to move on is NOW. You deserve better! Many women put themselves down so low that it ends up driving men away. You must love yourself better than that. How can anyone love you the way you are, if you don't love yourself the way you are? Move on, become the woman you are within, full of potential—a woman who can get whatever she wants if she just puts her mind to it.

Notice that you can achieve anything if you put your MIND to it. Your emotions are what is holding you back, making you doubt and stand still in time. Because of your emotions, you cry, you are sad all the time, you remember and you wonder where he is, you feel somehow it's your fault, and so forth. Your emotions cannot lead you anywhere and that is why you feel stuck.

Use your spirit—your MIND—and think straight. You've learned your lesson, now move on and do better next time. Let the past stay there and be useful only as an experience that taught you some valuable lessons in life.

God has been waiting for you all along. He wants to make you into a woman who will fit perfectly with the man He has prepared for you. Why waste your time on something that has already shown so much insecurity? Move on so that your future may finally unfold. Or don't, and let your emotions rule your life.

Notes

_____

_____

_____

_____

_____

_____

_____

_____

_____

_____

_____

_____

The Love Letter

The first time I laid eyes on you was back when things were so simple. You were young and everything was new for you. We never had enough of each other. The days were like hours and hours like minutes when we were together. Sometimes, we didn't even need to speak; just being together was enough and so precious. Oh, how I loved hearing your sweet voice, so gentle to my ears. And now, it has become so complicated somehow... it's not that I've changed, but things don't seem to be the way they were in the beginning.

I waited and waited for us to spend those hours together, to talk and listen to one another when time just did not matter, but I got tired of waiting. It has been so long since I've heard your sweet voice. The last time I spoke, you were not gentle at all, demanding this and that from me as if I were the one blocking your life. Why have you forsaken me, my beloved? Haven't I shown you enough of my love? What else must I do or say for you to understand how important you are to me?

Some days I search and search for you, but it seems you are always too busy to stop and see me. I was there when things didn't turn out well for you at your work place; nevertheless, you didn't bother to even look in my direction. I tried to talk to you whilst you were by yourself in your room the other night, but you immediately thought of watching TV instead.

I have noticed you visit my house once or twice a week, but more often than not, I feel as though you're not there for me at all. You come and go while things still don't change between us. Please don't get me wrong, I want things to change and I've been trying as hard as anyone possibly could, but these days you're so distant and indifferent to my voice, how else can I reach you?

I have loved you so dearly and now my Heart is broken for there are signs everywhere telling me this love is not mutual. It hurts, my beloved... I haven't stopped loving you though, and I've been waiting for your come back. I know you more than anyone else in your life and whatever is going on within you will soon rise to the surface and you'll finally realise what's really important in life. I'll wait. No matter how long it takes. I'll wait, for I've been praying for you and deep down I know you still long for the relationship we once had, it was strong and so innocent, nothing like any other relationship you have had or will ever have.

Perhaps things changed because we have never really touched. Our relationship was building up to that but when I was about to reveal everything about myself and show you a whole new life ahead, you stepped back. Not to worry, my beloved, there's still time for us to be closer than ever before, just let me know when you're ready and I'll come running. I'll place my ring on your finger and we'll declare our new life together forever and ever, and everyone will witness our love, true love. Therefore, it is worth the wait—I'll wait.

"O my dove, in the clefts of the rock, in the secret places of the cliff, let me see your face, let me hear your voice; for your voice is sweet, and your face is lovely." (So. 2:14)

Notes

_____

_____

_____

_____

_____

_____

_____

_____

What Do Women Want?

"It is so hard to understand women," many men say. It is as if we were a strange being from somewhere in space that needs a lifetime of research to figure out. And still, many die without truly understanding what women want. They make jokes as if we were this complex being that is almost impossible to please—but are we really? Is it so extraordinarily hard to please a woman?

If men could only see the amazing beings we are, they would not have a hard time understanding us at all. We are not as complicated as we seem to be, it's just that we are very emotional beings contrary to men, who are more rational. Women are more sensitive because of their inclination to their emotions.

Women have the ability of feeling each other's pain. We can actually feel sad just because of the sadness of someone else and this explains why we cry at the movies. Often men look at us in that sad moment of the movie and think we are so weak-minded, but that's not how it is. If they could only see what we are feeling in our flesh, what is going on there...

All we want is a little understanding—that's all! Understanding that we are more emotional than men and that means we need attention. We need to be loved in a way that will make our high maintenance heart fulfilled. Some men think they can show their love by bringing money home and giving us a roof over our heads—but that is so far from what we really want.

Women want the attention they so eagerly work for. Make-up, hair-dos, diets, success and talents we have are just a few signs of how much we wish to have our men's eyes on us. We will take hours to get dressed for this very reason. We will close up and quiet down just so our men can come and ask, "What's the matter?" We won't call and disappear from the map a while just so someone will ask, "Where were you?"

It may seem childish and even pathetic, but that is how we were made—emotional beings fuelled by attention. We love independence and yet we crave for the protection and security of marriage.

We love being considered equal to men in society and yet we are eager for the consideration and respect that was customary in the old days.

If any men can understand this much about women, they can say they understand women!

Notes

_____

_____

_____

_____

_____

_____

_____

_____

_____

_____

_____

_____

_____

_____

_____

_____

Ten Things Husbands Should Know About Their Wives

Sometimes we hear men talking about how complicated women are, and I wonder if those men who think this way really know women at all. So I decided to list some of the most common things (that I know of) women wish for in their husbands:

1. Little things are the ones that count the most. To be provided with a place to live, food to eat, and a marital status is just not enough. A woman misses it dearly when her man doesn't show his love for her in small but important gestures.

Women, in general, do not look at the whole picture, but instead, every single detail counts.

2. Withdrawal and change in mood are often signs of her need for attention. It may seem that she is cold and indifferent, but what she really wants is her husband to notice her.

She may be thinking that he is not appreciating her enough and is really trying to get him to come to her aid. It seems that she is not in the mood for love but what she really wants is more love.

3. Women want to be heard. They crave their husband's full attention in matters that mean the world to them, even though they are of no interest to their husbands.

Very often a woman will talk about anything just for the sake of having her husband listen to her. It is surprising how many wives feel lonely even though they have a husband by their side every night.

4. Women love to be noticed. They may dress for success and they will feel great, up until the point they realise that their husbands don't take notice of them.

Every time she looks at her man, she still sees him the same way as when she saw him for the first time; and that is how she wants him to see her, no matter her age or size.

5. A woman often wants spontaneity from her husband. Routine is boring in a marriage. A husband's spontaneous decision to take his wife out for dinner one day will be remembered by her for as long as she lives.

Just a little hint: wives love to be kissed, as when dating. It somehow makes them feel younger and still desired.

6. Wives love when their husbands put their foot down. They may not say so, but they surely appreciate having a head in the family. A man that does not use his authority in the house brings shame to his wife.

7. Women want their husbands to take the initiative. They love when their husbands make the first move and sometimes they actually try to see how far their husbands will go to please them. I know, we can be very complicated!

8. Wives crave appreciation from their husbands for the hard work they do taking care of the house and children. A simple "thank you" will do wonders for her at the end of the day.

9. Wives admire when their husbands are hard-working and faithful employees; when they are serious and determined to be successful in what they do. A coward or loser is what a woman dreads the most in a man.

10. In truth, the one thing that comes before all the above for a wife is her husband's fear of God. A woman feels secure when her man is a man of God. Nobody else in her family may be of God, but if her husband is, she is a happy wife.

Notes

How to Keep a Marriage

Sacrifice. No marriage can work without this attitude from at least one of the spouses. This is the problem of many couples that try to solve their problems by merely talking about them. They are willing to fight, they're willing to feel ashamed, they're willing to expose themselves, and they're willing to stay apart, but they're not willing to sacrifice—to let go of their ego and pride.

Sacrifice is by no means easy. It requires a lot of self-denial and determination. It sometimes makes a woman cry and feel like she's going nowhere, as if she is losing out for some reason. It leads her to ignore common sense and all that is right to this world just for one purpose, one goal, and one target—to save her marriage.

Humiliation will be one of the paths she'll have to take, but that is okay because the end result will be well worth it. A good marriage is all she's ever wanted in life since she was little girl, and she is determined to do whatever it takes to keep it. She will have to ignore everybody else's opinions too, because no one knows how determined she is to save her marriage.

Her friends don't understand her and even criticise her for 'living in the dark ages'. Her relatives will tell her to leave this nonsense marriage. And her inner self will often make her feel like a fool every time she gives up something in order to save her marriage. Sacrifice is everywhere, in every decision she makes, in every word she hears, and in every emotion she feels.

The woman who goes through the path of sacrifice stays married for life. People admire her marriage, a rare find nowadays. "They're so together and so alike" they think, but if only they knew how much sacrifice this couple have had to go through to be where they are now.

Marriage is one of the greatest blessings a woman and a man can have and because it is so good, it is expensive and never on discount. Few people are willing to pay the price and so few are those who truly enjoy the blessing of having a true marriage. Most people wait for a bargain and I am sorry to say they are still waiting and will continue waiting until they die. They will never find true happiness in marriage if they are not willing to sacrifice—to lose for a day or for some time in order to gain later.

I wish I could say that prayer alone is enough—but it's not. Not even God can do what you have to do in your marriage. Through prayers and the practice of the Word of God, God can bless, give you strength, and touch your husband's heart, but He cannot sacrifice on your behalf. It is your sacrifice and no one else's!

Notes

_____

_____

_____

_____

_____

_____

_____

_____

_____

_____

_____

_____

_____

_____

The Helper

"And the Lord God said, 'It is not good that man should be alone; I will make him a helper comparable to him." (Gen. 2:18)

There's much controversy on the subject of why and on what grounds we women were created. It is unfortunate that so many women, especially those who call themselves Christians, don't recognise their true role as wives. Some are rude to the extent of saying that our beliefs are from the dark ages when women meant nothing in society. I can understand their frustration, after all, they don't really know their Creator, so how can they acknowledge their role?

When God created the woman, He was very specific about her role in His Word. He created her with the purpose of being a helper to man. Her aim in life would be to suit and help her husband all the days of his life. She was made with as many qualities as possible so that she could assist him in every way. Emotional, sensitive, caring, thoughtful, gracious, kind, beautiful, strong, helpful, are just a few of her qualities.

It is not because God prefers man or that men are better than women. Don't allow this evil thought to confuse you about your value before God, as He said once, *"For you are all sons of God through faith in Christ Jesus... There is neither Jew nor Greek, there is neither slave nor free, there is neither male or female; for you are all one in Christ Jesus."* (Gal. 3:26 - 28)

Both men and women are special before God. The only difference between them in God's eyes is their role towards Him. The man's role is to glorify Him and the woman's role is to help her husband glorify Him. They both have the same aim—to glorify God—but with different and interdependent roles.

Imagine if in a school all the teachers would only teach about one subject? How could this team of teachers make a difference in a child's life? One must be able to teach Maths and the other must be able to teach English. They are both important for us, even if their roles are different. Both have the same aim and yet different roles.

That is what marriage is about—a team with only one goal—to glorify God, as two are much better than one! A single man and woman can glorify God but when they find their other mate for life, they can glorify Him much more. Not only because two can do more but also because one can help the other.

We wives must wake up every morning and think "How can I exercise my role is this marriage today?" or "How can I help my husband glorify God today?" When a wife knows her role, God blesses her. This does not only apply to women married to men of God also to women married to men who are not yet with God. A husband who is not of faith needs his wife's help even more because she will be God's tool to lead him to salvation.

Wives—fulfil your role and you'll fit into God's plan for your life.

Notes

_____

_____

_____

_____

_____

_____

_____

_____

_____

_____

_____

_____

One Body

So you know what is the hardest obstacle for a woman to overcome after marriage? If you're single, you'll do well to know about that before you get married. If you're married, you've probably thought of a list of things already. Adapting? Sacrificing? Accepting? Enduring? One word says it all: submission.

"There she goes again," you may say. Yes, I know we're in the 21st century and yes, I know women have changed over the years, and yes, I know we're equal to men. But submission has nothing to do with these things. You should be a modern woman, and by all means, do everything you've always dreamed of. There's nothing wrong with that, unless submission is not part of your life, and then you have a problem.

Man is the head and woman is the body. Fair, why not? One has got to be the body or it'll be two heads with no body, I don't think we want that. The head leads the body into doing whatever it wants it to do and the body gladly obeys it. And unless the body has some disability or the head is not mentally stable, both work pretty well together, don't you think? My body is not angry at my head and my head is not bitter with my body, on the contrary, my body loves doing what my head tells it to do and my head loves taking care of my body and would never harm it in anyway. As a matter of fact, my head sacrifices so my body can be comfortable and vice versa.

This is the idea behind marriage. When God created marriage, His intentions were to establish man as the authority in the marriage, not to diminish women, but to care for them. He knows that when this rule is followed properly, the husband always ends up doing his wife's wishes; after all, it's his pleasure to make her happy.

It's a pity though, to see so many women challenging their husbands as if they don't need a head. They can't picture themselves submitting to a man and so they have everlasting conflicts in the marriage—can't anyone wake up to the fact that it's clear where the problem is? How can a body, which is supposed to be one, have two heads and not function from the neck down?

The Bible is full of references about this secret of success in marriage and yet, people insist on ignoring it. They think their lack of submission is taking them somewhere—well, in fact it is, but probably not where they thought they were going! It's in man's nature to feel responsible for his wife and when he feels his place in the marriage threatened by a sense of independence or feminism, he becomes a frustrated husband. And I don't blame him.

The husband was the first authority God established in this world—before bishops and pastors, presidents and governors, and all other authorities you consider. And that's not all, he was made in God's likeness, as if saying, our husbands represent God to us. We, on the other hand, were made in man's likeness, from man, for man (Genesis 1.26; 1 Corinthians 11:7). We're not less than they; we're just made from the creation and not from the Creator. Does that mean anything to you? Your husband is a representative of God in your house and when you don't submit to him, you're challenging God Himself—forget about those offerings and prayers.

Notes

_____

_____

_____

_____

_____

_____

_____

_____

A Wife's Place

*M*any marriages end in divorce because of a common problem I call "confused roles". The husband lives selfishly for his ambitions and dreams whilst the wife wants to control everybody's life at once—hers, her husband's and her children's and that is when this marriage and family become chaos.

God teaches us in His Word about this:

"Wives, submit to your own husbands, as to the Lord. For the husband is head of the wife, as also Christ is head of the church; and He is the Saviour of the body. Therefore, just as the church is subject to Christ, so let the wives be to their own husbands in everything." (Eph.5:2 - 24)

To submit is not to become a slave or a doormat, but to allow our husbands to make the final decision. After all, imagine if there weren't any prime ministers, presidents, managers, supervisors, directors, and all those who are responsible to give a final word on any matter in this world? There would be mayhem everyday, everywhere, all the time!

The wife is portrayed as the church, which is the body. The body is subject to the will of the head. It works in submission to whatever the head decides and wishes. When it is sick, the head also gets sick. When it is cold, the head also gets cold.

The same applies the other way around. When the head is happy about something, the body jumps and dances. When the head wants something, the body sacrifices itself to get it. One needs the other and that is the mystery of Genesis 2:24, "Therefore a man shall leave his father and mother and be joined to his wife, and they shall become one flesh."

To be one is to be in understanding, in accordance, and in peace with each other and not the contrary. Many wives do not understand this and end up miserable and incomplete. And if that wasn't enough, their children grow up having the same anger and unbelief about marriage. No wonder there are so many young teenage girls getting pregnant nowadays.

Once a lady sent me a very frank e-mail saying that it was easy for me to say such things because I am married to a man of God, but how could she be this kind of wife if her husband is always drunk and never brings money home? Well, what about that other passage in 1 Peter 3:1,2, "Wives, likewise, be submissive to your own husbands, that even if some do not obey the word, they, without a word, may be won by the conduct of their wives, when they observe your chaste conduct accompanied by fear."

And this fear is not being afraid of your husband, but having fear of God in your heart to practise His Word as a good wife, mother and homemaker. A husband who watches his wife doing everything he is NOT doing, will eventually feel guilty and will start changing his behaviour towards her as well. I've seen this happen many times.

True marital happiness does exist and is out there for those who are willing to sacrifice their own desires and pride in order to fulfil their proper role.

When both husband and wife know their place in marriage, everything falls into place and they become the happy couple they had always dreamed of being when they first laid eyes on each other.

Notes

_____

_____

_____

_____

_____

_____

Is There a Limit to Submission?

"If your husband does not let you have any friends, would you just have to submit to this? If he keeps asking you to take out credit and never helps you repay any of it, would you have to submit to this? If your husband hurts you physically, would you have to submit? If your husband depends on you to go to work and do all the housework, would you have to submit? If your husband makes you sit in the bedroom by yourself every time his friends come over because he doesn't want you to see them, would you have to submit?" These were questions sent to me one day by what seemed to be a very sad and frustrated wife and due to the many similar e-mails I get regarding how far a wife should submit to her husband, I think it's time to write something about it.

It is a fact that submitting to a husband can many times be very hard, especially if he does not resemble our Lord Jesus in any way. However, an unbelieving husband needs his wife to be Christian enough in order for him to eventually become a man of God himself. He needs to be able to see something different about her from every other woman in the world and what can that difference be? Her love? Many other women in the world can even die for love! Her beauty? I don't think so. Her friendship? Isn't that something anyone can give? Her difference is exactly the one thing we're talking about: Her submission. No other woman in the world can submit, except those who live the Word of God.

Now that does not mean that the wife should submit to the point of getting hurt, leaving her faith, or even destroying her husband. We cannot obey God and leave Him at the same time. There are limitations as to how far you as a wife should submit, and this I say not to contradict the Word of God but to fully enlighten it. God never meant for us wives to be treated as slaves or diminished human beings. He is not a cruel God to make us do things in order to get hurt or even killed. We must know God in order to understand His Word. He created the woman to be man's helper.

If your husband hurts you physically, it is your obligation to get him help by reporting him to the police. It might sound like you're getting him into trouble, but you're actually helping him change. Imagine if you don't report him and he keeps on doing this, until one day, he actually kills you—won't he get into bigger trouble for that? Or for instance, He doesn't work and you're the breadwinner. If he's not working because of a situation out of his hands, that is fine, it's your duty to assist him in anyway you can, but if he's not working because he's just too lazy, you're not assisting him in any way if you're paying all his bills and providing everything for him. Stop this nonsense and get tough! Not with words of course, but allow him to get into a desperate state so he may go look for a job.

So you see, we are to submit, but not to be foolish with submission and destroy our own faith in God or even our husband's. Submit for helping purposes, otherwise your submitting may destroy everything altogether.

Notes

The Underlay of Marriage

*B*eing intimate with someone is sharing everything that you are with that person. It's beyond just a physical relationship—it's giving yourself to someone else. This kind of relationship is essential in marriage and should never be taken for granted. It is unfortunate to hear about married couples in the church that do not fully enjoy this area of their marriage.

I cannot stress enough how important this area of the marriage is. It is the base of your entire relationship. If it's not doing well, nothing else in your marriage will be doing well! The union and friendship between a couple depends pretty much on how intimate they are, and though some women think that this subject is not relevant because it is of the "flesh", I wonder where they got this idea since the Bible encourages this in 1 Corinthians 7:4-5:

"The wife does not have authority over her own body, but the husband does. And likewise the husband does not have authority over his own body, but the wife does. Do not deprive one another except with consent for a time, that you may give yourselves to fasting and prayer; and come together again so that Satan does not tempt you because of your lack of self-control."

As you can see, God prefers that you not fast rather than deprive your husband. Your intimate life with your husband is something God created in order to make you both become one. God wouldn't have created something evil or fleshy.

When this is practised within marriage it is indeed a blessing. Both husband and wife feel closer to each other, making the marriage alive instead of a routine thing. Any problems or issues that arise, they overcome easily because of the strength of this bond between them. They wake up in the morning ready for the day ahead, neither one of them can wait to see each other again and again, and the older they get, the closer they are (contrary to what most people think). Their eyes can only see each other because they live a fulfilled life.

When the wife is wise and understands the importance of intimacy in her marriage, she is never too tired or too busy for her husband. Instead, she prepares herself for this special time of day to spend with him making it a time to look forward to everyday. The more they know each other, the more attached to each other they get, making it very hard for anything or anyone to get in between them.

A husband who is fulfilled in his marriage will be fulfilled everywhere else in his life, but the contrary is sadly true as well. Husbands, who are not fulfilled in this area, are very frustrated husbands and easy prey for the devil's temptations. You must strive to succeed in your marriage, giving it the best you've got, after all, if this is the base of your marriage, shouldn't it be immaculate?

"Marriage is honourable among all, and the bed undefiled." (Heb. 13:4)

Notes

_____

_____

_____

_____

_____

_____

_____

_____

_____

_____

The Most Important Issue For a Wife

There's something every husband should know about his wife's needs. And no, it is not an endless list of jokes about how we are so hard to please. It is something husbands already have inside of them, but simply don't know how to use: LOVE.

To tell his wife he loves her and that's why he married her, does not mean much to her. To pay all the bills and come home every night is still not enough. One of the main teachings the Bible gives regarding husbands is exactly to "love their wives" as in Ephesians 5:28, *"So husbands ought to love their own wives as their own bodies; he who loves his wife loves himself."*

This verse describes pretty much the kind of love every wife wants: the love that cares for, protects, is gentle and kind, and above all, understands. Isn't that what every man does for his own body? How many men eat to the point of obesity just to satisfy their stomachs? Others, very concerned about their looks, spend hours in the gym. Many will go into debt just to buy a nice suit. In so many ways men show their love for their own bodies and yet, don't know how to love their wives.

Love is an everyday thing, just like a man loves his own body and takes care of it daily, so should his love be for his wife. It's not that she expects too much, it's just that she expects what she was promised. Remember your wedding vows?

God created women to suit and complete men and in turn, men to take care and give her all the love, protection, and attention she needs. Many wives lack this kind of love from their husbands and live wondering what they've done wrong. The minute they're alone with each other is the minute he'll use to watch TV, read a book, or play on PlayStation (would you pleeeez grow up?). Then later on, in the last few moments of the day, when they could enjoy each other, he's too tired. No wonder many husbands don't understand their wives—they don't even try!

A woman can truly complete a man, but if there's no love from his side, she'll feel incomplete and consequently unable to fulfil him. For a woman, love is as simple as one plus one is two. It's in her nature to love and that is why the Bible doesn't really emphasise the need for wives to love their husbands. But for a man, love can sometimes be forgotten or left aside. He loves but just doesn't take the time to show it.

Some husbands don't understand why it's so hard for the wife to get along with his relatives. But how can she, if she is not seen as his first love, but the love that comes after mother, father, brothers and sisters? The wife wants to be first (after God, of course). And God agrees with her. He said right in the beginning of creation, "Therefore a man shall leave his father and mother and be joined to his wife, and they shall become one flesh." (Ge. 2:24)

In short, the most important issue for the wife is that love is apparent in all that her husband does and is for her. If that is not apparent, it's not enough.

Notes

_____

_____

_____

_____

_____

_____

_____

_____

_____

_____

Pushing the Limits

It's time to go home and he immediately remembers his once lovely wife with that long face as he left for work this morning. He feels tempted not to go home tonight again, and this temptation is getting stronger by the day as things don't ever seem to change. He remembers how different she was when they just met. She was the woman of his dreams and falling in love with her was sudden. "What happened to that love we once shared?" he wonders, but there's no answer.

The wise Solomon, married to a thousand women, once said that a contentious wife is like a continual dripping (read Proverbs 19:13). Can you hear that irritating noise of the continuous dripping of a tap? One of the things that is surely guaranteed to get on a husband's nerves is your bad temper. A man can go through many problems and survive them all with the strength of his ego, but a difficult wife is a challenge most men can't match.

The wife, on the other hand, most assuredly does not recognise how difficult she is. She thinks that she has always been like this and that if he loves her truly, he must get used to her. Besides, deep inside, all she wants is for him to see his mistakes and humbly apologise for them. But the problem is that he doesn't see them and he can't clearly understand what she wants from him.

So they keep on living this marriage in irritation mode. She couldn't care less how his day was and he devotes all his time at home watching TV until his eyes can't take it anymore. She hates it that he doesn't ask what's wrong with her, and he hates to have to go home and see her long face day after day. Until when? That is the million-dollar question.

It is clear that both are wrong and that both need to change. However, I am here writing to women and so those who have ears to hear and eyes to read, read on!

Put yourself in his shoes. Are you a pleasant wife to go home to? If not, how can he take an interest in you or be eager to spend time with you? Your long face most probably will not do the trick. In fact, it will just make matters worse. Your husband, like most husbands, probably cannot see the signs you try so evidently to show. He's not psychic and his skills in understanding women are usually very low, because let's face it, we are very difficult sometimes.

Do you want to know the secret to change this situation in your marriage? Simple. Just change. If you change, he'll change. If you don't change, he won't change. I know, it's not fair but that is how it works. And once he changes, you'll be the happiest wife in the world, and that is not due to his change only, but mostly due to his desire to please you for being such a great wife. He'll get to the point of spoiling you, believe me!

No wonder the Bible says in Proverbs 14:1, *"The wise woman builds her house, but the foolish pulls it down with her hands."* Notice that it doesn't say MAN but WOMAN. When you push him to the limits, you're actually pulling your house down with your bare hands.

Notes

_____

_____

_____

_____

_____

_____

_____

_____

_____

From Mars?

*O*f you can only understand a man's nature, you'll have anything you want as a wife. He'll spoil you, making you the happiest woman alive. The problem is that many women think men are from Mars.

You've tried to talk to him, but he won't listen. You've tried to make him see, but he won't, making you feel completely shut out of the world he lives in. Thus the reason why there are so many books about this subject. People try and try to understand each other and often won't because it is not about psychology or studies, it's about man's nature—how he was created.

In Genesis 2:18-24, you can read about how the first woman was created. Adam with an exceeding joy couldn't help but show it with words such as, *"...This is now bone of my bones and flesh of my flesh..."* (Ge. 2:23)

It is interesting to note that although man is created in the image of God, the woman was created out of man. That should mean something for us women. If you're a mother, it's understandable to expect the child who was born from you to naturally respect you, even knowing that you're full of faults and that you don't know everything there is to know. It's absurd for any mother to be disrespected by her own children; now that's where your husband is coming from when you, his wife, "bone of his bones," disrespects him. In his concept of manhood, this is absurd.

Imagine yourself being made to complete a man and instead of doing that, you pull him apart from all that makes him special such as his manhood, leadership, and his being the head of the family?

The image your husband had in mind when he married you was to have someone by his side that would share life with him as his lifetime partner. And the image that you probably had in mind when you married him was to have someone who would take good care of you. Now how can he take care of you if you do not respect him? How can you be his lifetime partner if it's so hard for you to accept anything he says?

Husbands who do not have this understanding from their wives live out of place somehow, as if they are just not doing what they're supposed to be doing. Many end up looking for other things in order to fulfil this inadequate feeling. Some immerse themselves in the gym or in some kind of sport, others in their work, and still others just look for other women who will see them differently.

I understand how difficult it is to submit sometimes. I've been there myself. I remember a particular time when I made a choice not to say anything. I knew that he was wrong and that I had all the reasons to argue with him, but I simply decided to submit and let God honour me in my obedience to His Words. Later on in the day, it felt as if my husband owed me something. He tried everything to please me and I felt like a princess. But if I had made the other more obvious choice, the one that seemed more reasonable at the time, I wouldn't have been spoiled with attention later on. I would have only got into more problems and arguments.

That is why the Bible says, *"The wise woman builds her house, but the foolish pulls it down with her hands."* (Pv. 14.1)

Notes

Changing the Hubby

You married this man you love so much, but he's got a few things here and there that need changing. You've tried talking to him, but the more you talk about it, the less he changes as if he wants to stay this way just to get back at you. And you wonder if it is possible at all to change your husband.

Consider what you know already: talking does not do the trick! You've done it over and over again but as you can clearly see, it doesn't work. In fact, it can even make matters worse, as some husbands go to the point of doing the one thing you hate even more, just so you will give up telling them what to do.

In order to get through to your husband, you've got to change first. You'll only reach him when you have changed into the person he needs you to be. And when that happens, your husband feels obligated to change as well. This is the secret of every blessed marriage. The wife changed first and because of her change, her husband changed, too, and they lived happily ever after.

It is so simple and yet so difficult for people to understand. There are always those who think that it's so unfair, and that the only one who needs changing is the husband. That is why there are few couples that truly live a happy marriage. Some live for appearance and others are clearly unhappy with each other. No one likes changing—no one likes sacrificing. It's tough but that's the price for good things in life.

As long as you wait for him to change, he will be waiting for you to change, and things will remain as they are, and most probably get worse with time. These are the times we must remember that we are adults. Children are often the ones that think this way. The "You give me, I'll give you, but if you don't give me, I won't give you" attitude is simply too childish to bring into such a serious thing as marriage.

Your husband can still be the man of your dreams if you just use your wisdom, and with it shine so that his shine may also brighten up your lives. God needs you to get through to him, but how can God use a wife who is more stubborn than her own husband? How can He be glorified in a wife that is always nagging, and doing things with a long face? Think of how to use your intelligent faith, because that's the only way you'll see results.

Notes

_____

_____

_____

_____

_____

_____

_____

_____

_____

_____

_____

_____

_____

_____

_____

_____

_____

_____

Whatever That Means

W omen are constantly misunderstood by men and vice-versa. This is not a general statement but a fact and the reason for that is not because one is from Mars and the other from Venus, but because we were created differently so that one would complete the other.

You can never complete a puzzle when all pieces are the same. Although each piece of a puzzle fits together, they're always different from each other. That is the beauty of marriage. We're both very different from each other and yet we were made for each other.

There are ways we can be understanding, even when not understanding the other completely. This is the most difficult task in a marriage. Once you overcome this task, everything else is a piece of cake. Some couples take years to get to this stage and some end up getting divorced because they feel incapable of ever understanding the other. But there are steps one can take in order to make the whole process easier to achieve, which I list below:

1. Put yourself in his/her shoes—It's easy to criticise someone when you don't know what is going on with them. Many husbands expect more than their wives can handle at home; wives expect all their husband's attention, when all he can think about is how he'll be able to afford their monthly rent. If you can put yourself in the other's shoes, doing what the other is doing, going through whatever the other is going through—you'll probably be able to understand each other much better and consequently help instead of making demands.

2. Let go of your pride—This human characteristic is basically the primary one for unhappiness in love life. One's pride or ego impedes him from seeing his own mistakes, it doesn't allow time to

forgive, it keeps grudges forever if necessary, and never seeks reconciliation. In order for you to be happy, this is one of those things that you must let go—just bin it! Marriage with pride does not work, never did work, and never will work. If you want to understand your spouse—this is the first task on your to-do list.

3. Be honest and talk—Don't expect the other side to come around and start the whole conversation about what just went wrong between you two. Be the first to talk—bring up the matter at hand and put it all on the table. You will only understand things when they're out in the open. Don't expect your partner to automatically know what went wrong. Husbands expect their wives to notice how they've disappointed them, whilst wives can't even realise what they've done wrong and wives on the other hand expect their husbands to notice that they're not happy. Be honest and let your partner know how you feel.

4. The T factor—Be conscious of the appropriate time to ask or talk to the spouse. No matter how much he loves you or vice versa, you will argue for nothing if the subject was brought up at the wrong time of the day or even on the wrong day. Be wise and know when to talk about financial affairs or things you need or wished you had. Many are those who couldn't wait until the next day and ended up alone for the rest of their lives.

5. Give God a chance—He understands you both—enough said.

Notes

_____

_____

_____

_____

_____

_____

_____

_____

Frustrated Wives

Women, who have been devastated by their husbands in some form or another, go through life in frustration and traumatised by marriage. Their will in life is no longer to please their husbands but to live for themselves, which in a way, seems the best option considering what they have been through. By the time they hear that their role as wives is to please their husbands, it's almost too late for them to accept and live by it, for all they have experienced in marriage is abuse and disturbing behaviour.

Some are abused verbally and some even physically. They end up paying for their husbands' failures in life and uncontrollable addictions. The worst hour of the day is the time their husband arrives home, as they try hard to predict his mood. And a far worse scenario is the one the children witness before their very eyes. The wife can't help but feel humiliated and abused.

I cannot understand how these women feel, as much as I try, I will never know, for their experience in marriage has been far different from the one I have had. Although marriage wasn't always a bed of roses for me, I must say I was never devastated or frustrated by it. Instead, my marriage experiences have helped me become more mature and even closer to God. So I try to help with as much as I can from the Word of God, for that is the only source I find to be 100% accurate.

But still, there are wives who don't think that the Word of God is applicable to modern life and they question it as if it was an outdated book from the 1800s. Their frustration continues day after day without a remedy and the only visible solution is divorce. Would that be it? Would God create an institution so holy with so many flaws in it? Why do some marriages work and others don't?

The solution to marriage problems is never divorce, because if that were so, we could also say that the solution for a terminally ill person would be to kill him! Nobody ever kills someone because he's going to die. Instead, some use their faith in order for that person to be healed, others use hope, others go to the other side of the world to find a cure, others do research on finding a cure, and others spend as much time as possible with the one who is ill before his death.

When God created marriage, it was meant to be a covenant between a man and a woman. They would both live together and become one for as long as they lived. It was not meant to be trouble-free, of course. Compare it to our covenant with God: It requires a lot of self-denial and perseverance, but it's worth it. We have everything that God offers us in return.

The same thing goes for the covenant of marriage. If there is self-denial and perseverance, both will avoid many troubles and misunderstandings in their relationship.

Notes

_____

_____

_____

_____

_____

_____

_____

_____

_____

_____

_____

_____

_____

A Wife's Typical Mistakes

It is not as easy as it seems to go from being an independent, single woman to a wife. Many women can't wait for the day when they'll be wearing that long white dress and be seen as the most beautiful bride ever. But marriage is much more than just a dress and having someone to go home to.

Marriage is a bond that should not be broken. A bond that will last until the day you die. But I have seen many young couples struggle to get this bond working in their marriage. It is as if all their dreams of a happy marriage were dreams yet to come true.

There are eight typical mistakes we wives ought to know and avoid below illustrated in a humorous way [please don't be offended or take it personally if you have the same name as any of these]:

1. The Critical Catherine. Many wives like to criticise their husbands for being too this or that, for not being like someone else's husband and so forth. As much as they think they're only trying to help, that is not how their husbands (who tend to feel inferior by the words of the woman that knows him best) see it. The opposite works much better—if you praise him once in a while, his ego will start letting him do things he thought he could never do, and that is how a woman builds her man up.

2. The Lazy Laura. This kind of wife does not like her duties in the house. She hates feeling like a domestic worker for her husband, who in turn doesn't help out anywhere or on anything in the house. A good housewife will not demand her husband to do what she is supposed to do. Imagine if he were to demand her to go and make money to support him and the family? It is true that many wives work as well as their husbands, but it is still their responsibility to make sure that their house is clean, that food is on the table, that

the clothes are clean, and that their intimate life is still active at the end of the day. Some husbands end up leaving their wives because other women can give them what their wives are too lazy to give.

3. The Sentimental Sarah. Every husband needs a strong wife—someone who is ready for anything, someone who will go through hard times as if going through good times. Women who are too sentimental can often make their husbands feel frustrated and alone. These women will cry over anything. If they are rebuked, expect the overflow of the River Thames! The husband will often deal with this kind of wife as if handling a crystal glass. And that ends up becoming a burden for the rest of his life.

4. The Moody Margaret. This woman is like the waves of the sea. One minute she is up, the other she is down. One minute she is going to the right, the other she is going to the left. It's hard to live with such a person because you never know when she will be okay. Her difficult mood scares her husband off. When he thinks of her during the day, he doesn't think about how nice it would be if she were there with him, instead he wonders what he can find to do after work so he won't have to return home so early.

5. The Jealous Janet. This woman is jealous of anyone who comes near her husband, even his own parents. When a woman shows jealousy about her man, she immediately shows her insecurity about herself, and that is a weak spot no man likes to see. As mentioned before, husbands like to have strong wives, women who are secure enough to go through anything and still stand at the end of the day. A wife should by all means take care of her man, but not to the point of having the sinful feeling of jealousy.

6. The Angry Andrea. This is a constantly irritated woman. Anything that is said or done can easily push her buttons. An angry woman makes everyone around her feel uncomfortable. As the Bible says: *"Better to dwell in the wilderness, than with a contentious and angry woman."* (Pr. 21:19) She is avoided by many and still thinks people are not understanding. Little does she know that this is not anyone's problem but hers, and hers alone.

7. The Independent Ingrid. This woman thinks she does not need her husband's existence except for social situations where it will

look better for her to be beside a man. Her life is usually a mystery for her husband who constantly wonders why he got into this trap and became a white elephant in her life. Marriage is about unity. Unity of minds, of desires, of ideas, of everything you can think of. When one of the spouses does not understand the fact that they have now become one body, it is very hard to call it a marriage as it clearly doesn't serve the purpose.

8. The Busy Bianca. This is that wife who is always too busy with everything that is not related to her husband. Some wives get so busy with their work and with their children that they end up putting their marriage on hold. How can a woman be too busy for the most important part of her life? How can your children be happy and fulfilled if their parents have broken up? How can your work succeed and make you rich, but lonely? How can your charitable work towards others mean anything if the ones closest to you are the most needy?

Many wives suffer because of their own mistakes and if they only changed their behaviour and attitudes, they would see so much fruit come out of their marriage. Prayer alone will not do it. We have to act wisely. Act and pray.

There have been many husbands coming to church and being saved because of their wives' change of behaviour at home. It is exactly how that old Bible verse says: *"Wives, likewise, be submissive to your own husbands, that even if some do not obey the word, they, without a word, may be won by the conduct of their wives."* (1 Pe. 3:1)

Notes

_____

_____

_____

_____

_____

_____

The Working Woman

One of the most needed skills for a working woman is the ability to handle both her job and housework at the same time—and still look great at the end of the day.

Not many women can manage a busy lifestyle. They either work, work, work and look horrible or they look great but don't get much done in a day. And this can be a costly mistake because how can God bless her in everything she does if she is not doing everything to become a blessing?

There must be a balance. Balance is a must for everything in life, and it is applicable to all areas of our lives: spiritual, financial, romantic, emotional, family, and so on. I have lost count of how many women have approached me with problems due to their lack of balance in life. Everything becomes chaos and she loses control of her own life. But the woman of God is always in control. No matter how busy she is there is always time for God, herself, her family, and her work.

When God created the earth, He didn't do everything at once, neither did He take too long to get everything done. He took the proper time for everything and still had time to rest. Now, if God Himself had to have time to rest, imagine us human beings? Everything He created was good and perfect. Nothing was incomplete or done in such a hurry that it could have been better.

As His children, we should be able to do the same in our lives. Everything that we do should be good and perfect. Nothing should be done in a hurry so that we can later look back and feel frustrated about how it could have been so much better. And that includes: Our relationship with God, our health, our marriage, the raising of our children, the care of our home, and our work.

Our relationship with God is often disturbed by the much work we have, which ends up taking our time from coming to church, reading the Bible, and even praying to God. Many women think that they can remain strong spiritually if they only keep away from sin, but that is a trap Christians fall into. The less you go to church, the less you want to go. All of a sudden, you'll be going only twice a week, and then only once. Later on, you'll exchange that one time you dedicated to God for something else in your life, and before you know it, you won't be going at all. No wonder there are so many defeated Christians nowadays. They think they've reached a point where they don't really need to fight or pray anymore. How unwise they are!

Our health is another area that we tend to forget about. How can we be good Christians, wives, and mothers if we are sick? Always have a check up at the gynaecologist; this is a must for every woman. Don't delay in seeking treatment for small pains here and there, these could get worse and you could suffer for careless—not only you, but your whole family.

"How can I cope with everything at once?" is the question in many women's minds. Somehow, we are trained to think that we have too much to deal with in our lifetime and that men could never cope with the pressures we go through at work and home.

It is not that God created us to be slaves of time but we were carefully measured to fill in the gaps that men have, such as looking into details, seeing things ahead of time, organising time, and bringing out the beauty that's around us. Now, if we don't fill in those gaps, we end up feeling out of touch, or should I say, clueless. That is why it is important that we have full control of all aspects of our lives.

Our marriage comes right after our salvation. It's not a post or social status, it is a real commitment and bond between two people. Many women take this area for granted and only come to their senses after their husbands have already run off with someone else. Nothing and no one should replace the time you have to dedicate to your husband. If the Bible instructs us to serve our husbands as the Lord Jesus Himself, it does point out how important it is in our lives. There may be situations that will disturb your marriage, such as children and relatives getting in the middle of both husband and wife. The woman of God will never allow anyone or anything to get between her and her husband. When a marriage is not doing well, nothing else will—why neglect such a sensitive part of your life?

The raising of our children is also very important. To be a mother is not to give the children something to eat, a place to sleep, and clothes to wear. To be a mother is to be there for our children in every way. When work takes this quality time away from our children, they grow into something we'll regret later on. They start having problems in school and we'll just have to deal with it later on. It is no use praying for them if we are not there for them.

The care for the house can sometimes be a burden for some women. They work so much during the day and when they arrive home for their "second job", they just feel too exhausted to move a finger. The consequence will usually be: anything for dinner, loads of clothes inside a basket, a full sink, not much space to sit on the sofa, not much floor space to walk on, not much space to place anything else on the counter! Do you think that the Lord Jesus would ever live in such a house? Can you represent God in any way to your guests? Can you feel the presence of God this way? I don't think so. When the Bible talks about the House of God, the Temple, and the Presence of God, it describes it in many beautiful ways and one of them is CLEAN! But when it talks about the devil, it even calls evil spirits UNCLEAN spirits. Can you now realise why it is so important for you to include your house duties in your weekly schedule?

I know by experience that to be in control is not easy but I also know that it is possible and if you apply yourself, you will be the working woman that will glorify God.

Notes

_____

_____

_____

_____

_____

_____

Dream House

Think about the most reputable and beautiful High Street store you know. Now think about the least popular and least attractive store that you can. What's the difference between the two besides price?

Families take the day out just to go and visit the best one. Any gift from such a store can really make a person happy. People talk about it, other stores envy it, and still it gets more and more beautiful every time you go in.

A beautiful home is like this beautiful store. You feel pleasure to come home at the end of a tiresome day. And there are those days that you just feel like staying in and ordering a take-away. When you leave, you even look back and admire it once again. You know where everything is because it is your home, your own space, and your hiding place from the crazy world outside.

It is rare to find such a home nowadays. Landlords have a hard time fixing the house after the tenant's leave at the end of the lease. Kids will do anything to go and stay over at somebody else's home. Teens can't wait to grow up and leave. Husbands feel tired and exhausted but still manage to go straight from work to the pub. Wives dislike staying in during the day. And so this family goes in and out of this not so lovely home everyday.

The secret of a lovely and beautiful home (besides the presence of God in it) cannot be found in home decorating items. It's something very basic, simple, and yet undesirable to many. It's called cleanliness. Now think about that popular store again and you will realise that:

1. The beautiful one is clean and tidy, while the other is quite grubby.

2. The beautiful one is carefully decorated, while the other is very ordinary.

3. The beautiful one pulls you in even if you don't have money, while the other makes you look away.

Why is it clean? You wonder. Well, anything clean and tidy catches our attention. There are those streets that you feel like taking a picture in, and those that you feel like running away from and catching the tube ASAP.

Why decorated? The decoration reveals the kind of store it is. It gives you a portrait of beauty and why else would you buy anything there?

Why does it pull you in? Well, beauty is still an attraction to many!

If cleanliness is so important in the streets and in the places we go, how much more is it for our homes!

Many families plan their finances around the dream of having their own house. Yet when it is acquired, they still can't see the image they had in their minds. They have the best house, live in the best neighbourhood, have the best furniture, and still don't have this cosy and pleasant home they always dreamed of. And why? Exactly because they don't think the subject of cleanliness is important.

A good housewife will keep her house clean and tidy on a daily basis. She makes sure that it is cosy for her family to enjoy coming home to. Her children enjoy bringing their friends in. Her guests love going to visit her. Her home becomes her own portrait, beautiful and delightful. After all, isn't that part of her role at home?

Notes

_____

_____

_____

_____

_____

Time for Children?

Most women want to have children and some even say it's their calling, but few of them think of the right time to have them. They are so concerned about having children before a certain age that they completely ignore the circumstances in which they are bringing a child into this world. When little importance is given to the right time to have children, misfortune comes without delay.

Many parents have problems just because they decided to have children at the wrong time in their life. Problems that extend into their marriage. When you see a little baby in his mother's arms, the picture itself is great. There seems to be so much love and caring there, you feel tempted to get one of those for yourself. The truth is that having a little baby to carry around is not quite as simple as it may seem.

I remember when parents used to be the most important people in a child's life. Today, children can't wait to leave home. They easily badmouth their parents to others and their attitude towards them is often aggressive and disrespectful. Mothers were once the most beautiful women in the whole world, but nowadays girls only want to know about pop stars. Fathers used to be the man their son looked up to; nowadays, they are ashamed of them.

If you're ready to go through all the hardships of having children of your own, you must first be prepared to deny your own selfish reasons. Have the right motives for having children—bear them for God. If you think that your children will be yours to keep, you're 100% mistaken. They will be yours to care for and raise, but just for a while and that is why the wisest reason to have children is to have them for God—so they may serve God with their lives. Your goals for your children will not be to have this or that, but to be of God and serve Him with their lives. This is the only way they'll be safe.

Now here's a list of times to avoid having children:

1. You've recently gotten married. It's time for you to know your husband well and to dedicate 100% to your marriage. Having a child now will disrupt your adjustment to this marriage and will consequently occupy all your time and efforts that could otherwise be given to your partner.

2. You're having problems in your marriage. Be wise and solve your marital problems first before bringing an innocent child to be part of the problems and grow up feeling revolted at seeing so much strife in his family.

3. You're struggling in your finances. That means you'll end up leaving your child with others so that you can work overtime, and that is when children start relying on the wrong crowd, drugs, video games, and TV to raise them. Be financially stable first so that you can be there to raise your child.

4. You're depressed. If you're not well spiritually, your child won't be either. Your mood and your temper are always passed on to your child. Work on your spiritual life first by making sure you're fit for the many battles you'll need to face when raising children.

Notes

_____

_____

_____

_____

_____

_____

_____

_____

_____

Your Child's Dad

No, this article is not about your husband, partner, or the guy that left you pregnant years ago. Every child that is born into this world has the same common parent, thus the reason why sometimes you feel as though all the love and care you give is just not enough. The same evil things attract them all: lying, deceiving, stealing, cheating, and everything of that sort.

How can an innocent little baby after only a few years of life behave like a little monster? How can daddy's little princess dress so sluttish only to go to school? Why is it so hard for mama's boy to open up to her and not lock himself in his room all the time? We have only this child's other parent to blame, you know, the one called the "world".

Every child born immediately becomes another fruit of this world, another child whose inclinations are all contrary to what is good and is of common sense. They are more inclined to listen to other problematic kids than their own mother and father. They will do anything in their power to be like everyone else and become popular, no matter how ridiculous they walk or dress.

Kids are no longer children nowadays. Years and years ago, children still had the decency of respecting their parents and profited more by spending their time playing with toys and outdoor games. Today, if they don't have a video game or access to the Internet, their life is 'soooooo boring'.

I used to think that a child was God's gift to us, but I've come to realise that, unfortunately, God had nothing to do with this choice we made. I remember complaining to Him about my son, and how I wasn't going to accept raising a child for the devil's praise, but I didn't realise at the time that it wasn't God who made me a mother.

I demanded his blessing upon my child and yet, years would come and go, and Filipe would still bring me sadness instead of honour. It was only when I realised that what I was going through was a fruit of my own choices that I stopped feeling so frustrated as a mother and started asking God for help. Today, I'm happy to say he's become the child I asked God for. I know that soon he'll be serving God even more with his life, but that's just a matter of time.

Our child is our sole responsibility. And if we are finding it hard to raise him, we must call for God's help and direction. There isn't a manual on how to raise a child. Every child is different and inasmuch as some methods work on some, most children simply need a more customised method, and that is where God comes in. If you have tried everything you could think of to raise your child and you realise that it is not working, it's now time to turn to God and be humble to ask for help.

Just like with everything else in our lives, God can fix it. We were also raised by this world and did things we are ashamed of. By our own doing, we got ourselves into many problems, but one day, we came to God and He fixed our lives and became our True Father. Children will only really change when they become true children of God. Meanwhile, pray for them. And if you still don't have a child of your own, do think before having one. You'll be bringing one more child to this corrupt world. It's a big gamble.

"But woe to those who are pregnant and to those who are nursing babies in those days! For there will be great distress in the land and wrath upon this people." (Lk. 21:23)

Notes

_____

_____

_____

_____

_____

_____

Being a Mum—It's About Them

So you want to be a mum? Every time you see a little baby in its mother's arms you desire it even more. I am going to ask some hard questions here for want-to-be mums: Why do you want to be a mum? Is it because they're cute? Is it because it will be fun? Is it because you can show your baby to others? Is it because you want to keep your partner? Is it because you're lonely? Is it because you want to know what it's like? Is it because you can get government benefits? Is it because you want to ensure your surname continues after you die? Why do you want to be a mum? If you had to undergo a test in order to be authorised to be a mother, do you think you'd pass?

Motherhood is a full-time job with long hours and extra time. It's not a task for just anyone and I would even say that it is one of the most important jobs in the entire world. You are bringing another human being to life—can you feel the weight of responsibility? And if that wasn't heavy enough, you'll be making yourself responsible for him for the rest of your life. Whoever he becomes, he'll still be your son. Whatever she does, she'll still be your daughter, and that is a very heavy weight to bear. You will be directly responsible for teaching your child everything he needs to know in order to succeed. Now, if you haven't learned that yourself yet, it's going to be tricky!

You may think that every woman is meant to be a mum and therefore it is a natural thing, but think again: how many mums actually succeed in raising their children the right way and making them be the best they can be? If women in society today automatically knew how to be good mums, life would definitely not be the way it is today—children killing other children, kids taking drugs, teenagers getting pregnant. Now I ask you that question again: how many mums succeed? Not many. Some adults have a hard time finding their place in the world just because of the way they were brought up. Now that must mean something.

Every woman wants to be a mum, but can everyone really be one? You don't have to go to college for a motherhood degree, but you must be aware of what you're getting yourself into. You cannot have children and just let them be raised by TV, the Internet, school, friends, and so forth. You brought them in to the world so now you must take care of them—full stop.

If the reasons you're having children are any in the first paragraph of this article, you're having them for the wrong reasons and, therefore, you'll be greatly disappointed. You see, if you could not fulfil the above requirements, how can a little child fulfil them for you? Isn't it unfair to expect your little baby now to ensure your partner stays home? Or for him to take your loneliness away, making your life more fun? How can your baby do that?

Notes

_____

_____

_____

_____

_____

_____

_____

_____

_____

_____

_____

_____

The Honour They Want to Give

$\mathcal{I}$ was only 10 when I started playing the piano, and I wasn't much into it back then. But every time I heard my father say how nice it would be if I could play the piano for him some day, it would just drive me to learning it better every time. I wanted to impress him, to make him proud of me, to honour him somehow—and every time I played it, my father would come close to me and give me a kiss and that would just make my day. Often I would play only to get that kiss and when he didn't show up, I felt like all my playing was in vain. In fact, I didn't even play it when he wasn't home.

After we grow up, the same feeling is always there in the back of our minds. "How will my father react about this in my life?" or "What does my father think of me?" or even "Would this impress him today?" It's hard to give it up, although we know we have to; after all, we're now a grown up and many of us already parents ourselves. But still, we crave to hear them say, "I'm so proud of you!" It feels as if we're still children.

The fact is that children have this desire deep within, and they carry it on with them as teenagers, then as adults. And though they often do everything to displease or even hurt their parents, the truth is that many of them are just hurting inside. They tried for a couple of years, maybe even their whole life to hear something nice about them from their parents and since all they've heard were harsh words and evil labels, they decided to grab on to these bad names and make them real in their lives.

Every time we parents call our children names, we're actually making them believe that they are that way. If you went through this, you know how hard it was for you. All you wanted in life was to make your parents proud of you but when you realised that you were doing the opposite, no matter how hard you tried, you decided you might as well just fulfil their prophecy about you.

Every child has his/her own good qualities and weaknesses, just like every parent and every human being. We make mistakes, we are often stubborn, and therefore tend to make the same mistakes over and over again. Now imagine if you had someone you loved the most in your life all the time saying, "What a failure you are!"

Our children naturally want to make us proud. As parents we should allow them to, but not in our own way or in what we feel we'll be proud of, but in the way they can make us proud.

Just as God is not harsh or even critical of us, but is always giving us a second chance and reassuring us of His unconditional love, so should we be with our children. Let them honour you, it's in their blood—and it's in your blood too.

Notes

Mummy's Tasks

eing a mother is not an easy task. There are special tears that only mothers shed. I look at this child, full of life ahead of him, depending on the kind of mother I am in order to enjoy its fullness, and I gather that his life is literally in my hands. This pure and gentle child needed me to be his mother and love him in such a way that he could become a better person than I ever was and not have to go through the hardships that I have gone through in my life. This is what my son needs from me, and this is the task of every mother.

It is unfortunate that many of us think about having children for the wrong reasons. Some of us want to have them because we are lonely and would love to have a child around. I remember having this desire early on in my marriage. Some want to have them in order to keep a relationship going. And worst of all, there are some who have them because of all the government benefits they can have. One reason worse than the other, but all have one thing in common: the mother is just thinking about herself.

A mother who gives birth to children in order to satisfy one or two of her needs will eventually be angry at them for not fulfilling her expectations and consequently will raise them the wrong way. Little does she know that if she, who is an adult already, could not fulfil her own needs, how can children do it? It is completely unfair and that is why many of these children grow up to be rebellious teenagers, full of anger inside towards their parents.

When I first laid eyes on my son, I set a goal for him—not a goal for me, but a goal for him. I remind myself of that goal everyday and, therefore, I do my best in order to be the mother he needs me to be. I cannot be the mother my mother was for me because as a child, I had different needs. I cannot be the mother people tell me to be because only I know the kind of mother my son needs me to be. That does not give me the right to impose my way on him, but only to be what he needs me to be. He gave me his life and therefore I must fulfil my task of motherhood.

Sometimes the government has to take drastic measures and actually remove a child from her parents' custody. This happens because many children who entrusted their lives to their parents lived in abuse from the start. We cannot blame the government for removing children from their own parents when many of these children have actually been saved because of this law. However, it is up to you and me to know well what motherhood is all about. It's not about us—it's about our children!

Notes

_____

_____

_____

_____

_____

_____

_____

_____

_____

_____

_____

_____

_____

_____

_____

Mother Christmas

$\mathcal{I}$t is interesting to note how some women can actually portray "Mother Christmas" during the final months of the year. From November onwards, their agenda is filled with plans and ideas for Christmas. When December finally arrives, they're running up and down getting gifts for everyone they know, buying Christmas cards for people whom they have never even met, and getting their Christmas decorations up for a cosy Christmas day with the family.

I remember someone in my family who used to be in charge of getting the Christmas party ready for the whole family to participate in. On Christmas day, the food was always spectacular and the decorations were original and well planned. And if that wasn't enough, she always had gifts for every nephew and niece, and I was one of them. I loved the idea that she always remembered me on Christmas day and so it was always very exciting to go to her house for Christmas.

However, for some reason that I didn't know at the time, she wasn't my favourite aunt. The aunt I most felt comfortable with had been unemployed at the time and hardly ever gave me any gifts, even on my birthdays. I really liked her because she used to spend time talking to me and teaching me things that no one had the time to. I felt really special when she'd come by, as if she was really glad to see me. She was happy when I was happy and sad when I was sad.

Whilst one gave me all the best gifts, the other gave me love and attention. That is exactly what happens to many children nowadays. Many mothers and aunts try their very best to impress at Christmas, forgetting that all it takes to impress their children, nieces, and nephews is the simple act of giving them something MasterCard cannot buy: LOVE.

One may try to give you gifts and even make you feel special on Christmas day, and still not be as loved as someone who actually makes you feel special every other day of the year. Love shouldn't be shown only by the giving of gifts but by smaller and more effective ways such as an encouraging word on a dreary day, a hug out of the blue, a kiss of "Hello, how nice to see you", and a smile after a long day of work.

The time you spend with your child is more memorable to him than the tons of gifts you give him. The moments you take just to sit down with him and talk to him about his day at school is more valuable than you think. The little things that we forget about are the ones that really make the difference in all kinds of relationships, including friendship and marriage.

This year, don't just give gifts to your loved ones—spend precious time with them. Give them a smile when they wake up and a hug when they go to sleep. Tell them how important they are for you on a given day. Let them know you love them unconditionally and that might just make this year the best they ever had.

Notes

_____

_____

_____

_____

_____

_____

_____

_____

_____

_____

_____

_____

True Discipline

Being a mother myself, I know how badly we mothers want to effectively discipline our children so it will have a positive effect later on in their lives. We try all kinds of methods we hear from our own mothers and friends, but it is still very hard to pinpoint which way is best.

True discipline certainly does not make a child grow up to be rebellious or angry with you but it makes the child grow up to thank you for his or their childhood. So what is the true discipline we mothers must make sure we give our children?

We know that our children are all different and that we cannot expect that one rule will work for all. But there are everyday things that we mothers can do that will affect any child. I list them below:

1. Get involved with your growing child. Don't let your child grow up to be whatever he becomes. Get involved in his growth. Make sure that you work on those weaknesses in character and behaviour that can really harm your child. Perhaps he lies constantly, and you think that this is just a temporary period of his childhood, but I tell you it's not. Whatever bad behaviour or attitude in your child that is not corrected by you, will stay within him for the rest of his life.

2. Mould your child. Make your child the person he or she dreams to become. I've heard parents say of their child, "That's the way he is"—as if parents have no influence on their children. We can make our child be whoever we want him to be. Of course that we'll have to work on them constantly, but it's possible to mould our children the way we want them to become.

3. Lead your child to become the man or woman he or she longs to be. And by that I don't mean career wise. Maybe your child always dreamed of becoming a pilot, but in reality, he didn't want to become a pilot just so he could fly planes and earn lots of money, he wanted to become a pilot so he could impress you. So that's what you have to work on his character for him to impress not only you but most of all, himself.

4. Spend time with your child. Your child may love to be with other children or spend time in the park, but it is more important that you spend time with him than to give in to his wishes. Spending time with other children is good for him but is not as good as spending time with you.

5. Seek God for guidance. You don't need to be religious to have His guidance in your life. God is the best Father there is and you can really learn some good lessons from Him. I did!

Notes

_____

_____

_____

_____

_____

_____

_____

_____

_____

_____

_____

_____

_____

_____

Rebels by Nature

There was a time when children brought their parents so much pride and respect that couples had loads of them. Families consisted of many members, when nowadays most children only have one other sibling. Unfortunately, one of the reasons why many parents prefer fewer children is because they know with almost prophetic certainty that their children will grow up under the influence of a rebellious generation.

Today, many parents are afraid of their own children because their attitude problems extend to the point of physical abuse. They speak to their parents as if they were less than their own pet and they never listen to them as they do to strangers, whose advice most of the time is so wrong.

In order for us to deal with a problem so deep as rebellion, we must first understand its root. Rebellion was the first sin in the world, long before man was created and it happened right before God's eyes in heaven. Lucifer was a very powerful angel in heaven, very close to God, who decided one day to stop giving God all the honour and glory. Lucifer wanted to be like God, and in his own understanding, led a rebellion with a host of other angels. And that was when evil was born.

God had no choice but to expel him and his followers from heaven, after all, they were contaminating many other angels. And that is exactly what rebellion does first. It contaminates others. Children, contrary to the title we've used for this article, are not natural rebels. If you remember them when they were small, it was easy for you to tell them things and get them to trust you in every way. The problem is that as they grow, the rebellious attitudes of others start to creep in to their innocent minds and it doesn't take long before they are completely contaminated.

Rebellious attitudes and thoughts are in schools, among neighbours, on TV, and in music. And aren't these the staple diet of children nowadays? They just have to have that video game, to watch that TV show, to listen to that kind of music, and befriend those kinds of kids. And there you go—you've got total contamination.

Many mothers keep blaming themselves for not having done enough for their children but that couldn't be further from the truth. The truth is that most of the time, the mother did her best. All she failed to do was to set some limits in order to avoid this tragedy. God in His great wisdom as a parent Himself, over and over again in His Word, taught us to stay away from evil.

Allowing your children to have whatever they wish and do whatever they wish is actually leading them to a path of rebellion. They need limits and most of them, if not all, don't have a clue how to set limits for themselves. They can't see evil coming, which is why we parents need to do that for them. Of course, we cannot hold them back from having friends or watching TV altogether, but we can surely monitor their friendships and their TV time. There's nothing better than to find profitable things for your child to do when they're not in school.

Someone once said, "The trouble with being a parent is that by the time you're experienced, you're unemployed." Let us not waste any more time. Let us take control of our own children so this evil may never take root in our families.

Notes

_____

_____

_____

_____

_____

_____

_____

_____

Beware—Teens in the Area!

She's rolling her eyes at you, practically saying to your face, "I can't stand you" and all you can do is count to 10 and remember all those friends' and relatives' comments about how you should expect this from your teenager. Why? Why should you accept this kind of disrespect from your own daughter? Why should you just wait and see what happens after this phase of her life is gone? You're both Christians, shouldn't it be different for you? Why do you have to go through the same hassle everybody else goes through?

I've said this and will continue saying it, though I've been criticised because of this many times: I don't see why I should accept that I have to go through the same struggles non-Christian parents do! It's just ridiculous! It's as if the child is old enough to do whatever he wants. But can you honestly accept the concept that teenagers know enough about life in this world to live on their own as they please? Of course not. They're teenagers, which means, they're at that stage just before adulthood. Whatever they do or don't do will greatly influence their adulthood.

If you as a parent allow yourself to be put down by your teenager, then you're giving him a very bad start in life. Soon, he won't be respecting anyone else, which will consequently be a block in his spiritual life—if he can't respect you, how can he respect God?

All that coming to church thing will be left in his past, and will mean nothing to him later on in life. This is the reason why so many children who were practically raised in the church live a life that makes you wonder what they were doing in church all their life. They are young adults full of depression, failure, and anger. They bring you shame every now and again, when your friends witness their indifference to God.

Let us be real parents, not just any parent. You see your child going the wrong way, grab his arm and get him on the right path whilst he's young and under your care. If later, as an adult, with his life under his own care, he decides not to follow your God, then you can at least say, "I've done my part." It's easier for a teenager who didn't grow up in church to convert than a teenager that was raised in the church.

I'd like to back this up with my own experience as a teenager. I was taught to respect both my parents no matter what. When I didn't do that, my parents didn't simply ign ore my disrespect—I was rebuked. And if I didn't like the rebuke, I was rebuked for that, too! That must have worked because I can't remember being a troubled teenager; in fact, I met God during my teenage years.

It's not about forcing our kids to believe in God and come to church. It's about making them understand they're just children—not better than their parents, not old enough to know what's best, and not wise enough to know all the answers. I don't force my son to do anything in the church, but on the other hand, I expect him to be the child he is and if he doesn't agree with that, tough—he'll just have to wait until he grows up!

Notes

_____

_____

_____

_____

_____

_____

_____

_____

_____

_____